THE 2024 VEGETARIAN AIR FRYER COOKBOOK UK

Healthy British Recipes with UK Measurements for the Ninja Dual Zone Air Fryer

ALMA D. GIBBS
Copyright © 2024 By ALMA D. GIBBS. All rights reserved worldwide.

No part of this book may be reproduced or transmitted in any form or by any means, electronic or mechanical, including photocopying, recording, or by any information storage and retrieval system, without written permission from the publisher, except for the inclusion of brief quotations in a review.

Warning-Disclaimer:

The purpose of this book is to educate and entertain. The author or publisher does not guarantee that anyone following the techniques, suggestions, tips, ideas, or strategies will become successful. The author and publisher shall have neither liability nor responsibility to anyone with respect to any loss or damage caused, or alleged to be caused, directly or indirectly, by the information contained in this book.

This copyright notice and disclaimer apply to the entirety of the book and its contents, whether in print or electronic form, and extend to all future editions or revisions of the book. Unauthorized use or reproduction of this book or its contents is strictly prohibited and may result in legal action.

TABLE OF CONTENTS

INTRODUCTION 5
ABOUT THIS COOKBOOK 5
BENEFITS OF VEGETARIAN AIR FRYING 6
CHAPTER 1: BREAKFAST AND BRUNCH 9
    Veggie Frittata Cups 9
    Tofu Scramble with Air-Fried Potatoes 9
    Air-Fried Avocado Toast with Tomatoes 10
    Vegetable Hash Browns 10
    Chickpea Flour Pancakes 10
    Air-Fried Veggie Sausage Patties 11
    Overnight Oats with Air-Fried Fruit 11
    Vegetable and Tofu Breakfast Burritos 12
    Air-Fried Veggie Quiche Bites 12
    Vegan French Toast Sticks 13
CHAPTER 2: APPETIZERS AND SNACKS 14
    Air-Fried Vegetable Chips (Potato, Beet, Carrot, Parsnip) 14
    Crispy Air-Fried Falafel Bites 14
    Stuffed Mushroom Caps with Breadcrumb Topping 14
    Air-Fried Vegetable Spring Rolls 15
    Spicy Roasted Chickpeas 15
    Baked Vegetable Samosas 16
    Air-Fried Jalapeño Poppers 16
    Zucchini Fritters with Tzatziki Dip 17
    Roasted Red Pepper Hummus with Veggie Sticks 17
    Air-Fried Veggie Meatballs 18
CHAPTER 3: SALADS AND SIDES 19
    Air-Fried Brussels Sprouts with Balsamic Glaze 19
    Roasted Cauliflower with Tahini Dressing 19
    Grilled Vegetable Salad with Balsamic Vinaigrette 19
    Air-Fried Sweet Potato Fries 20
    Baked Stuffed Tomatoes 20
    Air-Fried Vegetable Skewers 20
    Roasted Beet and Arugula Salad 21
    Crispy Air-Fried Kale Chips 21
    Grilled Corn on the Cob with Herb Butter 21
    Roasted Butternut Squash with Cranberries and Pecans 22
CHAPTER 4: SANDWICHES AND WRAPS 23
    Air-Fried Falafel Wraps with Tahini Sauce 23
    Veggie Panini with Pesto and Roasted Peppers 23
    Tofu Banh Mi with Quick Pickled Veggies 24

Grilled Vegetable and Hummus Wraps 24
Air-Fried Portobello Mushroom Burgers 24
Crispy Tofu Sandwiches with Sriracha Mayo 25
Mediterranean Veggie Pitas 25
Air-Fried Eggplant Parmesan Sandwiches...26
Vegan BLT Wraps with Tempeh Bacon 26
Roasted Vegetable and Pesto Panini 27

CHAPTER 5: SOUPS AND STEWS 28

Roasted Vegetable Soup with Air-Fried Croutons 28
Lentil and Sweet Potato Stew 28
Creamy Tomato Soup with Air-Fried Basil Croutons 29
Vegan Chili with Air-Fried Tortilla Strips 29
Curried Cauliflower Soup 30
Italian Vegetable Minestrone..30
Air-Fried Crispy Chickpeas for Soups and Salads 31
Roasted Butternut Squash Soup 31
Vegetable Noodle Soup 31
Air-Fried Veggie Meatballs for Stews...32

CHAPTER 6: VEGGIE MAINS 33

Air-Fried Tofu Steaks with Mushroom Gravy 33
Vegetable Fritters with Yogurt Sauce 33
Lentil and Vegetable Shepherd's Pie 34
Air-Fried Veggie Burgers 34
Stuffed Portobello Mushrooms with Quinoa 35
Vegetarian Meatless Meatballs in Marinara Sauce 35
Air-Fried Tofu Nuggets with Dipping Sauces 36
Vegetable Pot Pie with Biscuit Topping 36
Vegan Lentil Loaf with Cranberry Glaze 37
Roasted Vegetable Lasagna..37

CHAPTER 7: PASTA AND GRAIN DISHES 38

Air-Fried Gnocchi with Pesto 38
Vegetable Pasta Bake..38
Quinoa Bowls with Roasted Veggies 39
Air-Fried Vegetable Fritters over Pasta 39
Vegan Mac and Cheese 40
Lentil Bolognese over Zucchini Noodles 40
Mediterranean Couscous Salad 41
Stuffed Pasta Shells with Spinach and Ricotta 41
Air-Fried Veggie Meatballs with Spaghetti 42
Mushroom Risotto with Crispy Air-Fried Leeks 42

CHAPTER 8: PIZZA AND FLATBREADS 44

Air-Fried Veggie Pizza 44
Naan Bread Pizzas with Roasted Veggies 44

Flatbread Wraps with Falafel and Veggies 45
Air-Fried Calzones with Spinach and Feta 45
Grilled Vegetable and Pesto Pizza 46
Vegan BBQ Jackfruit Flatbread 46
Air-Fried Garlic Knots 47
Mediterranean Veggie Stromboli 47
Caprese Flatbread with Balsamic Glaze 48
Mexican-Inspired Veggie Pizzas 48

CHAPTER 9: DESSERTS AND BAKED GOODS 49

Air-Fried Fruit Crisps (Apple, Berry, Peach) 49
Baked Apples with Oat Crumble Topping 49
Vegan Banana Bread 50
Air-Fried Veggie Muffins (Carrot, Zucchini, Pumpkin) 50
Chocolate Avocado Mousse 51
Air-Fried Doughnuts with Fruit Glazes 51
Vegan Brownies 52
Air-Fried Cinnamon Sugar Churros 52
Raspberry Coconut Macaroons 53
Chocolate Chip Chickpea Cookies 53

CHAPTER 10: SAUCES, DIPS, AND CONDIMENTS 54

Air-Fried Veggie Dips (Spinach Artichoke, Pico de Gallo, Hummus) 54
Mango Chutney 54
Pesto Sauce (Basil, Arugula, Sun-Dried Tomato) 55
Vegan Ranch Dressing 55
Chipotle Cashew Cream Sauce 56
Tzatziki Sauce 56
Romesco Sauce 56
Vegan Cheese Sauce 57
Harissa Paste 57
Air-Fried Veggie Croutons for Soups and Salads 58

CONCLUSION 59

INTRODUCTION

Welcome to the World of Vegetarian Air Frying!

You're embarking on an exciting culinary journey filled with delicious, healthy, and incredibly convenient vegetarian dishes made possible by the magic of air frying. This revolutionary cooking technique has taken the world by storm, allowing you to enjoy crispy, flavorful foods without the need for excessive oil or unhealthy frying methods. By choosing a vegetarian lifestyle, you've already taken an important step towards improving your health, reducing your environmental impact, and exploring a world of vibrant, plant-based flavors. And with an air fryer by your side, you'll unlock a whole new realm of possibilities, transforming everyday vegetables, legumes, grains, and meat alternatives into mouthwatering masterpieces. Imagine biting into perfectly crisp Brussels sprouts with a tantalizing balsamic glaze, savoring the delightful crunch of air-fried falafel without the greasiness, or indulging in decadent desserts like warm fruit crisps and churros, all while keeping things light and guilt-free. The air fryer's rapid air circulation system creates a crispy, oven-baked texture using little to no oil, making it the ultimate tool for health-conscious cooking. But air frying isn't just about creating delicious treats; it's also an incredibly versatile technique that opens up a world of possibilities. From perfectly roasted vegetables bursting with natural sweetness to delightfully crispy veggie burgers and fritters, your air fryer will become your trusty sidekick in the kitchen. Preparing wholesome, satisfying meals has never been easier or more enjoyable.

This cookbook is designed to guide you through every step of your air frying journey, whether you're a seasoned vegetarian chef or a complete beginner. We'll start by exploring the principles of air frying, demystifying the appliance, and providing you with essential tips and tricks for achieving optimal results every time. Next, we'll delve into the world of vegetarian cuisine, celebrating the vibrant flavors and nutritional benefits of a plant-based diet. You'll learn about essential ingredients, flavor combinations, and meat alternatives that will elevate your vegetarian dishes to new heights. But the heart of this cookbook lies in the meticulously crafted recipes, carefully curated to showcase the best of what air frying has to offer. From hearty mains to light bites, indulgent desserts to nourishing salads, we've got you covered with a diverse array of crowd-pleasing dishes that will satisfy every craving.

Each recipe is thoughtfully designed with the beginner in mind, featuring clear instructions, helpful tips, and mouthwatering photographs to guide you along the way. We'll also provide nutritional information, enabling you to make informed choices and cater to specific dietary needs or preferences. Moreover, this cookbook goes beyond just recipes by offering invaluable insights into meal planning, prepping, and incorporating air frying into your daily routine. You'll learn clever time-saving techniques, batch cooking strategies, and innovative ways to repurpose leftovers, ensuring that your air fryer becomes an integral part of your healthy, sustainable lifestyle.

So, whether you're seeking to improve your health, reduce your environmental footprint, or simply explore new culinary frontiers, this "Vegetarian Air Fryer Cookbook UK" is your ultimate guide. Embrace the joy of air frying, and get ready to unlock a world of delicious, crispy, and nutritious meals that will tantalize your taste buds and leave you feeling energized and satisfied.

ABOUT THIS COOKBOOK

This "Vegetarian Air Fryer Cookbook UK" is more than just a collection of recipes; it's a comprehensive guide to unlocking the full potential of air frying while embracing a vibrant, plant-based lifestyle. Within these pages, you'll find a wealth of knowledge, inspiration, and practical advice designed to empower you on your journey towards healthier, more sustainable eating habits. At its core, this cookbook aims to demystify the art of air frying, providing you with a solid foundation to build upon. We'll start by exploring the science behind this innovative cooking technique, delving into the mechanics of how air fryers work and the principles that govern their operation. You'll gain a deeper understanding of the rapid air circulation system, temperature control, and the unique capabilities that set air fryers apart from traditional ovens and fryers. But this cookbook isn't just about the "how"; it's also about the "why." We'll dive into the numerous benefits of air frying, showcasing how this method can help you create deliciously crispy, golden-brown dishes with significantly less oil than traditional frying methods. You'll discover how air frying can be a game-changer for those seeking to reduce their intake of unhealthy fats and calories while still indulging in their favorite fried treats. Recognizing the growing demand for plant-based diets, we've dedicated a substantial portion of this book to celebrating the vibrant world of vegetarian cuisine. You'll embark on a culinary exploration of diverse vegetarian protein sources, from nutrient-rich legumes and tofu to versatile meat alternatives like tempeh and seitan. We'll also provide valuable insights into essential nutrients for vegetarians, ensuring that your meals are not only delicious but also well-balanced and nutritionally complete. One of the standout features of this cookbook is its unwavering commitment to catering to beginners. Whether you're a newcomer to air frying, a novice in the kitchen, or simply seeking straightforward, foolproof recipes, you'll find a wealth of user-friendly guidance within these pages. Each recipe is meticulously crafted with clear, step-by-step instructions, helpful tips, and beautiful photography to inspire and guide you every step of the way. But this cookbook goes beyond just recipes; it's a comprehensive lifestyle guide for those seeking to embrace air frying as a long-term, sustainable practice. We'll share invaluable meal planning strategies, prepping techniques, and time-saving hacks that will streamline your cooking process and make air frying a seamless part of your daily routine. Additionally, we understand that dietary preferences and restrictions can vary, which is why we've included a dedicated section on ingredient substitutions and modifications. Whether you follow a vegan, gluten-free, or any other specialized diet, you'll find practical advice and creative solutions to adapt these recipes to suit your unique needs. Furthermore, this cookbook recognizes the importance of culinary versatility and variety. With a diverse array of recipes spanning breakfast delights, appetizers, salads, sandwiches, soups, mains, pastas, pizzas, desserts, and even sauces and condiments, you'll never find yourself stuck in a culinary rut. Each chapter offers a tantalizing selection of dishes, catering to different cravings, occasions, and dietary preferences. But what truly sets this cookbook apart is its commitment to fostering a sense of community and shared experience. Throughout its pages, you'll find personal anecdotes, insider tips, and relatable stories that will make you feel like you're part of a vibrant, supportive network of fellow air frying enthusiasts. We recognize that cooking is not just a practical pursuit but also a creative outlet and a means of connecting with others through shared flavors and traditions. In essence, this "Vegetarian Air Fryer Cookbook UK" is a comprehensive resource that goes beyond mere recipes. It's a practical guide, a source of inspiration, and a companion on your journey towards healthier, more sustainable, and deliciously satisfying plant-based meals. Whether you're a seasoned vegetarian or a curious newcomer, this book will equip you with the knowledge, skills, and confidence to master the art of air frying and unlock a world of flavorful possibilities.

So, let's embark on this exciting culinary adventure together, embracing the joy of air frying while celebrating the vibrant flavors and nourishing goodness of a vegetarian lifestyle. Get ready to discover a whole new world of crispy, mouthwatering dishes that will tantalize your taste buds and leave you feeling energized, nourished, and deeply satisfied.

BENEFITS OF VEGETARIAN AIR FRYING

Embracing a vegetarian lifestyle and incorporating air frying into your cooking routine offers a multitude of benefits that extend far beyond just flavor and convenience. By combining these two elements, you're embarking on a path that promotes personal well-being, environmental sustainability, and a deeper appreciation for the vibrant flavors of plant-based cuisine.

Health and Nutrition: At the forefront of the benefits lies the positive impact on your overall health and nutrition. Vegetarian diets are inherently rich in fiber, antioxidants, and a wide array of essential vitamins and minerals found in whole, plant-based foods. By eliminating meat and animal products, you're reducing your intake of saturated fats and cholesterol, which can contribute to a lower risk of heart disease, certain cancers, and other chronic conditions.

Air frying takes this health advantage a step further by allowing you to enjoy crispy, flavorful dishes without the need for excessive oil or unhealthy frying methods. Traditional deep-frying can introduce significant amounts of calories, unhealthy fats, and potentially harmful compounds formed during the frying process. With air frying, you can achieve that coveted crispy texture using minimal oil, resulting in dishes that are lighter, healthier, and more nutrient-dense.

Environmental Impact: Adopting a vegetarian lifestyle and embracing air frying also has a positive impact on the environment. Plant-based diets generally have a smaller carbon footprint compared to meat-heavy diets, as they require fewer resources and contribute less greenhouse gas emissions during production. By reducing your reliance on animal products, you're playing a role in promoting sustainability and reducing the strain on our planet's resources. Furthermore, air frying is an energy-efficient cooking method that consumes less electricity than traditional ovens, contributing to a lower overall environmental impact. By minimizing the use of oil, you're also reducing the demand for oil production, which can have adverse effects on ecosystems and contribute to greenhouse gas emissions.

Flavor and Variety: Contrary to popular belief, vegetarian air fryer cooking is far from bland or restrictive. In fact, it opens up a world of vibrant flavors, textures, and culinary possibilities. By focusing on fresh, whole ingredients and embracing the natural sweetness and complexity of vegetables, grains, legumes, and plant-based proteins, you'll discover a newfound appreciation for the depth and nuance of vegetarian cuisine. Air frying enhances these flavors by creating a delightful contrast between crispy exteriors and tender, juicy interiors. From perfectly roasted vegetables bursting with natural sweetness to delightfully crispy veggie burgers and fritters, your air fryer will become your trusty sidekick in unlocking a world of vegetarian delights.

Convenience and Versatility: In today's fast-paced world, finding the time and energy to prepare nutritious, satisfying meals can be a challenge. That's where air frying shines, offering a level of convenience and versatility that is unmatched. With rapid air circulation and precise temperature control, air fryers can cook a wide variety of dishes in a fraction of the time compared to traditional methods, without sacrificing flavor or texture.
From crispy appetizers and sides to hearty mains and indulgent desserts, your air fryer can handle it all. And with the ability to cook multiple items simultaneously, you can effortlessly prepare complete, well-rounded vegetarian meals in a single appliance, minimizing the need for multiple pots and pans.

Cost-Effective: Adopting a vegetarian lifestyle and incorporating air frying can also be a cost-effective choice. Plant-based ingredients, such as grains, legumes, and in-season produce, are often more affordable than meats and animal products, especially when purchased in bulk or from local sources. Additionally, air fryers are generally more energy-efficient than traditional ovens, leading to potential savings on your utility bills over time.By embracing vegetarian air fryer cooking, you're not only nourishing your body and reducing your environmental impact but also potentially saving money in the long run. It's a win-win situation for your health, the planet, and your wallet.

Endless Possibilities: One of the most exciting aspects of vegetarian air fryer cooking is the endless possibilities it presents. With a diverse array of recipes spanning breakfast delights, appetizers, salads, sandwiches, soups, mains, pastas, pizzas, desserts, and even sauces and condiments, you'll never find yourself stuck in a culinary rut. As you explore the recipes in this cookbook, you'll discover innovative ways to transform familiar ingredients into extraordinary dishes. From crispy vegetable chips and falafel bites to decadent fruit crisps and baked treats, the possibilities are truly limitless. Moreover, air frying encourages creativity and experimentation, allowing you to adapt recipes to suit your personal preferences, dietary restrictions, or the seasonal produce available in your region. This cookbook serves as a starting point, but the true magic lies in your ability to make these recipes your own and continuously explore new flavors and combinations.

By embracing vegetarian air fryer cooking, you're not only nourishing your body but also cultivating a deeper appreciation for the incredible diversity and versatility of plant-based cuisine. Get ready to embark on a flavorful journey that will tantalize your taste buds, nourish your soul, and leave you feeling energized and inspired to embrace a healthier, more sustainable lifestyle.

CHAPTER 1: BREAKFAST AND BRUNCH

Veggie Frittata Cups

Prep: 15 mins | Cook: 15 mins | Serves: 4

Ingredients:
- US: 200g mushrooms (sliced), 1 red bell pepper (diced), 1 small onion (finely chopped), 100g spinach (chopped), 8 large eggs, 60ml milk, salt, pepper, cooking spray
- UK: 200g mushrooms (sliced), 1 red bell pepper (diced), 1 small onion (finely chopped), 100g spinach (chopped), 8 large eggs, 60ml milk, salt, pepper, cooking spray

Instructions:
1. Preheat your air fryer to 180°C (350°F).
2. In a bowl, whisk together eggs, milk, salt, and pepper.
3. Grease muffin tin cups with cooking spray.
4. Divide mushrooms, bell pepper, onion, and spinach evenly among the muffin cups.
5. Pour the egg mixture over the veggies, filling each cup about three-quarters full.
6. Place the muffin tin in the air fryer basket.
7. Air fry for 12-15 minutes until the frittata cups are set and lightly golden.
8. Remove from the air fryer and let them cool slightly before serving.

Nutritional Info (per serving): Calories: 140 | Fat: 8g | Carbs: 5g | Protein: 10g

Tofu Scramble with Air-Fried Potatoes

Prep: 10 mins | Cook: 20 mins | Serves: 2

Ingredients:
- US: 200g firm tofu, 1 tablespoon nutritional yeast, 1/2 teaspoon turmeric, salt, pepper, 300g potatoes (cut into cubes), 15ml olive oil, 1/2 teaspoon paprika
- UK: 200g firm tofu, 1 tablespoon nutritional yeast, 1/2 teaspoon turmeric, salt, pepper, 300g potatoes (cut into cubes), 15ml olive oil, 1/2 teaspoon paprika

Instructions:
1. Preheat your air fryer to 200°C (400°F).
2. Wrap tofu in a clean kitchen towel and press to remove excess moisture.
3. Crumble tofu into a bowl and mix in nutritional yeast, turmeric, salt, and pepper.
4. In another bowl, toss potatoes with olive oil, salt, pepper, and paprika.
5. Place potatoes in the air fryer basket in a single layer.
6. Air fry for 15-20 minutes, shaking halfway through, until crispy.
7. Meanwhile, cook tofu scramble in a non-stick skillet over medium heat until heated through.
8. Serve tofu scramble with air-fried potatoes.

Nutritional Info (per serving): Calories: 320 | Fat: 14g | Carbs: 30g | Protein: 18g

Air-Fried Avocado Toast with Tomatoes

Prep: 5 mins | Cook: 5 mins | Serves: 2

Ingredients:
- US: 2 slices whole grain bread, 1 ripe avocado, 1 small tomato (sliced), salt, pepper, chili flakes, lemon juice
- UK: 2 slices whole grain bread, 1 ripe avocado, 1 small tomato (sliced), salt, pepper, chili flakes, lemon juice

Instructions:
1. Preheat your air fryer to 180°C (350°F).
2. Mash avocado in a bowl and season with salt, pepper, chili flakes, and lemon juice.
3. Toast bread slices until lightly golden.
4. Spread mashed avocado on the toasted bread.
5. Top with sliced tomatoes.
6. Place the avocado toast in the air fryer basket.
7. Air fry for 3-5 minutes until the edges are crispy.
8. Serve hot.

Nutritional Info (per serving): Calories: 250 | Fat: 12g | Carbs: 30g | Protein: 6g

Vegetable Hash Browns

Prep: 15 mins | Cook: 20 mins | Serves: 4

Ingredients:
- US: 2 large potatoes (grated), 1 small onion (finely chopped), 1 small carrot (grated), 1/4 cup all-purpose flour, 1/2 teaspoon garlic powder, salt, pepper, cooking spray
- UK: 2 large potatoes (grated), 1 small onion (finely chopped), 1 small carrot (grated), 30g all-purpose flour, 1/2 teaspoon garlic powder, salt, pepper, cooking spray

Instructions:
1. Preheat your air fryer to 200°C (400°F).
2. Place grated potatoes in a clean kitchen towel and squeeze out excess moisture.
3. In a bowl, combine potatoes, onion, carrot, flour, garlic powder, salt, and pepper.
4. Form mixture into hash brown patties.
5. Grease air fryer basket with cooking spray.
6. Arrange hash browns in the air fryer basket in a single layer.
7. Air fry for 15-20 minutes, flipping halfway through, until golden and crispy.
8. Serve hot with your favorite dipping sauce.

Nutritional Info (per serving): Calories: 150 | Fat: 1g | Carbs: 30g | Protein: 4g

Chickpea Flour Pancakes

Prep: 10 mins | Cook: 10 mins | Serves: 2

Ingredients:
- US: 1 cup chickpea flour, 1 cup water, 1/2 teaspoon baking powder, 1/2 teaspoon turmeric, salt, pepper, 1 tablespoon olive oil
- UK: 120g chickpea flour, 240ml water, 1/2 teaspoon baking powder, 1/2 teaspoon turmeric, salt, pepper, 15ml olive oil

Instructions:
1. In a bowl, whisk together chickpea flour, water, baking powder, turmeric, salt, and pepper until smooth.
2. Heat olive oil in a non-stick skillet over medium heat.
3. Pour batter onto the skillet to form pancakes.
4. Cook for 2-3 minutes until bubbles form on the surface.

5. Flip and cook for another 2-3 minutes until golden brown.
6. Repeat with the remaining batter.
7. Serve warm with your favorite toppings.

Nutritional Info (per serving): Calories: 270 | Fat: 7g | Carbs: 38g | Protein: 12g

Air-Fried Veggie Sausage Patties

Prep: 10 mins | Cook: 15 mins | Serves: 4

Ingredients:
- US: 200g cooked lentils, 100g mushrooms, 1 small onion, 2 cloves garlic, 1 teaspoon smoked paprika, 1/2 teaspoon fennel seeds, salt, pepper, 30g breadcrumbs
- UK: 200g cooked lentils, 100g mushrooms, 1 small onion, 2 cloves garlic, 1 teaspoon smoked paprika, 1/2 teaspoon fennel seeds, salt, pepper, 30g breadcrumbs

Instructions:
1. In a food processor, combine cooked lentils, mushrooms, onion, garlic, smoked paprika, fennel seeds, salt, and pepper.
2. Pulse until mixture is well combined but still slightly chunky.
3. Transfer mixture to a bowl and mix in breadcrumbs.
4. Form mixture into patties.
5. Preheat your air fryer to 180°C (350°F).
6. Place patties in the air fryer basket in a single layer.
7. Air fry for 12-15 minutes, flipping halfway through, until golden and crispy.
8. Serve hot with your favorite condiments.

Nutritional Info (per serving): Calories: 180 | Fat: 2g | Carbs: 30g | Protein: 10g

Overnight Oats with Air-Fried Fruit

Prep: 5 mins | Cook: 15 mins | Serves: 2

Ingredients:
- US: 1 cup rolled oats, 1 cup almond milk, 2 tablespoons maple syrup, 1/2 teaspoon vanilla extract, 1/2 teaspoon cinnamon, 1 apple (sliced), 1 pear (sliced)
- UK: 120g rolled oats, 240ml almond milk, 30ml maple syrup, 1/2 teaspoon vanilla extract, 1/2 teaspoon cinnamon, 1 apple (sliced), 1 pear (sliced)

Instructions:
1. In a bowl, mix together rolled oats, almond milk, maple syrup, vanilla extract, and cinnamon.
2. Divide mixture into two jars or bowls.
3. Cover and refrigerate overnight.
4. Preheat your air fryer to 180°C (350°F).
5. Arrange sliced fruit in the air fryer basket.
6. Air fry for 10-15 minutes until fruit is caramelized and tender.
7. Top overnight oats with air-fried fruit before serving.

Nutritional Info (per serving): Calories: 300 | Fat: 4g | Carbs: 60g | Protein: 6g

Vegetable and Tofu Breakfast Burritos

Prep: 15 mins | Cook: 10 mins | Serves: 2

Ingredients:
- US: 200g firm tofu, 1/2 red bell pepper (diced), 1/2 green bell pepper (diced), 1 small onion (diced), 100g spinach, 2 large whole wheat tortillas, 1 avocado (sliced), salsa, salt, pepper
- UK: 200g firm tofu, 1/2 red bell pepper (diced), 1/2 green bell pepper (diced), 1 small onion (diced), 100g spinach, 2 large whole wheat tortillas, 1 avocado (sliced), salsa, salt, pepper

Instructions:
1. In a non-stick skillet, scramble tofu over medium heat until heated through.
2. Add diced bell peppers, onion, and spinach to the skillet.
3. Season with salt and pepper and cook until vegetables are tender.
4. Warm tortillas in the microwave or oven.
5. Divide tofu mixture between the tortillas.
6. Top with sliced avocado and salsa.
7. Roll up the tortillas into burritos.
8. Serve warm.

Nutritional Info (per serving): Calories: 400 | Fat: 15g | Carbs: 50g | Protein: 20g

Air-Fried Veggie Quiche Bites

Prep: 15 mins | Cook: 20 mins | Serves: 4

Ingredients:
- US: 4 large eggs, 1/2 cup milk, 1/2 cup grated cheese, 1/2 cup diced mixed vegetables (bell peppers, spinach, tomatoes), salt, pepper
- UK: 4 large eggs, 120ml milk, 60g grated cheese, 60g diced mixed vegetables (bell peppers, spinach, tomatoes), salt, pepper

Instructions:
1. Preheat your air fryer to 180°C (350°F).
2. In a bowl, whisk together eggs and milk.
3. Stir in grated cheese and diced vegetables.
4. Season with salt and pepper.
5. Grease muffin tin cups with cooking spray.
6. Pour egg mixture into muffin cups.
7. Place the muffin tin in the air fryer basket.
8. Air fry for 15-20 minutes until quiche bites are set and lightly golden.
9. Remove from the air fryer and let them cool slightly before serving.

Nutritional Info (per serving): Calories: 200 | Fat: 12g | Carbs: 6g | Protein: 14g

Vegan French Toast Sticks

Prep: 10 mins | Cook: 10 mins | Serves: 2

Ingredients:
- US: 4 slices whole grain bread, 120ml almond milk, 1 tablespoon ground flaxseed, 1 teaspoon vanilla extract, 1/2 teaspoon cinnamon, cooking spray, maple syrup (for serving)
- UK: 4 slices whole grain bread, 120ml almond milk, 1 tablespoon ground flaxseed, 1 teaspoon vanilla extract, 1/2 teaspoon cinnamon, cooking spray, maple syrup (for serving)

Instructions:
1. In a shallow bowl, whisk together almond milk, ground flaxseed, vanilla extract, and cinnamon.
2. Cut each slice of bread into sticks.
3. Dip bread sticks into the almond milk mixture, coating evenly.
4. Preheat your air fryer to 180°C (350°F).
5. Grease air fryer basket with cooking spray.
6. Place bread sticks in the air fryer basket in a single layer.
7. Air fry for 8-10 minutes until golden and crispy.
8. Serve warm with maple syrup for dipping.

Nutritional Info (per serving): Calories: 250 | Fat: 6g | Carbs: 40g | Protein: 8g

CHAPTER 2: APPETIZERS AND SNACKS

Air-Fried Vegetable Chips (Potato, Beet, Carrot, Parsnip)
Prep: 15 mins | Cook: 20 mins | Serves: 4
Ingredients:
- US: 1 large potato, 1 beetroot, 2 carrots, 2 parsnips, 15ml olive oil, salt, pepper, smoked paprika (optional)
- UK: 1 large potato, 1 beetroot, 2 carrots, 2 parsnips, 15ml olive oil, salt, pepper, smoked paprika (optional)

Instructions:
1. Preheat your air fryer to 180°C (360°F).
2. Peel and thinly slice the potato, beetroot, carrots, and parsnips into chips.
3. In a large bowl, toss the vegetable slices with olive oil, salt, pepper, and smoked paprika if using.
4. Arrange the seasoned vegetable slices in a single layer in the air fryer basket.
5. Air fry for 15-20 minutes, shaking the basket halfway through, until the chips are golden brown and crispy.
6. Remove the vegetable chips from the air fryer and serve immediately as a crunchy and healthy snack!

Nutritional Info (per serving): Calories: 160 | Fat: 4g | Carbs: 28g | Protein: 3g

Crispy Air-Fried Falafel Bites
Prep: 20 mins | Cook: 15 mins | Serves: 4
Ingredients:
- US: 1 can (400g) chickpeas, 1 small onion (chopped), 2 cloves garlic (minced), 30g fresh parsley, 15ml lemon juice, 30g breadcrumbs, 5ml olive oil, 5ml water, 5g ground cumin, 5g ground coriander, salt, pepper
- UK: 1 can (400g) chickpeas, 1 small onion (chopped), 2 cloves garlic (minced), 30g fresh parsley, 15ml lemon juice, 30g breadcrumbs, 5ml olive oil, 5ml water, 5g ground cumin, 5g ground coriander, salt, pepper

Instructions:
1. Drain and rinse the chickpeas, then pat them dry with a paper towel.
2. In a food processor, combine the chickpeas, onion, garlic, parsley, lemon juice, breadcrumbs, olive oil, water, cumin, coriander, salt, and pepper.
3. Pulse until the mixture is coarse but well combined.
4. Shape the mixture into small balls and place them on a greased air fryer tray.
5. Lightly spray the falafel balls with olive oil.
6. Air fry at 200°C (400°F) for 12-15 minutes, turning halfway through, until golden and crispy.
7. Serve the crispy falafel bites hot with your favorite dipping sauce!

Nutritional Info (per serving): Calories: 180 | Fat: 4g | Carbs: 29g | Protein: 7g

Stuffed Mushroom Caps with Breadcrumb Topping
Prep: 15 mins | Cook: 15 mins | Serves: 4
Ingredients:
- US: 8 large mushrooms, 30g breadcrumbs, 1 clove garlic (minced), 15g fresh parsley (chopped), 15ml olive oil, salt, pepper, grated Parmesan cheese (optional)
- UK: 8 large mushrooms, 30g breadcrumbs, 1 clove garlic (minced), 15g fresh parsley (chopped), 15ml olive oil, salt, pepper, grated Parmesan cheese (optional)

Instructions:
1. Remove the stems from the mushrooms and finely chop them.
2. In a bowl, mix together the chopped mushroom stems, breadcrumbs, garlic, parsley, olive oil, salt, pepper, and Parmesan cheese if using.

3. Spoon the breadcrumb mixture into the mushroom caps, pressing gently to pack.
4. Preheat your air fryer to 180°C (360°F).
5. Arrange the stuffed mushroom caps in the air fryer basket.
6. Air fry for 12-15 minutes until the mushrooms are tender and the breadcrumb topping is golden brown.
7. Serve the stuffed mushroom caps hot as a delicious appetizer or snack!

Nutritional Info (per serving): Calories: 90 | Fat: 4g | Carbs: 11g | Protein: 4g

Air-Fried Vegetable Spring Rolls

Prep: 25 mins | Cook: 15 mins | Serves: 4

Ingredients:
- US: 8 spring roll wrappers, 100g cabbage (shredded), 100g carrots (julienned), 50g bell pepper (julienned), 50g bean sprouts, 2 spring onions (chopped), 15ml soy sauce, 5ml sesame oil, 5ml olive oil, salt, pepper
- UK: 8 spring roll wrappers, 100g cabbage (shredded), 100g carrots (julienned), 50g bell pepper (julienned), 50g bean sprouts, 2 spring onions (chopped), 15ml soy sauce, 5ml sesame oil, 5ml olive oil, salt, pepper

Instructions:
1. In a large bowl, mix together the shredded cabbage, julienned carrots, bell pepper, bean sprouts, and chopped spring onions.
2. Add soy sauce, sesame oil, olive oil, salt, and pepper to the vegetable mixture and toss until well combined.
3. Place a spoonful of the vegetable filling onto a spring roll wrapper.
4. Fold the sides of the wrapper over the filling, then roll tightly into a spring roll, sealing the edge with water.
5. Preheat your air fryer to 200°C (400°F).
6. Lightly spray the spring rolls with olive oil.
7. Arrange the spring rolls in the air fryer basket in a single layer.
8. Air fry for 12-15 minutes, turning halfway through, until golden and crispy.
9. Serve the air-fried vegetable spring rolls hot with sweet chili sauce or soy sauce for dipping!

Nutritional Info (per serving): Calories: 180 | Fat: 4g | Carbs: 32g | Protein: 5g

Spicy Roasted Chickpeas

Prep: 10 mins | Cook: 30 mins | Serves: 4

Ingredients:
- US: 1 can (400g) chickpeas, 15ml olive oil, 5g ground cumin, 5g smoked paprika, 5g garlic powder, 5g chili powder, salt, pepper
- UK: 1 can (400g) chickpeas, 15ml olive oil, 5g ground cumin, 5g smoked paprika, 5g garlic powder, 5g chili powder, salt, pepper

Instructions:
1. Preheat your air fryer to 200°C (400°F).
2. Rinse and drain the chickpeas, then pat them dry with a paper towel.
3. In a bowl, toss the chickpeas with olive oil, ground cumin, smoked paprika, garlic powder, chili powder, salt, and pepper until evenly coated.
4. Spread the seasoned chickpeas in a single layer in the air fryer basket.
5. Air fry for 25-30 minutes, shaking the basket halfway through, until the chickpeas are crispy.
6. Allow the roasted chickpeas to cool slightly before serving as a crunchy and flavorful snack!

Nutritional Info (per serving): Calories: 150 | Fat: 5g | Carbs: 20g | Protein: 6g

Baked Vegetable Samosas

Prep: 30 mins | Cook: 20 mins | Serves: 4

Ingredients:
- US: 8 sheets phyllo pastry, 200g potatoes (peeled and diced), 100g carrots (peeled and diced), 1 onion (chopped), 2 cloves garlic (minced), 15ml olive oil, 5g ground cumin, 5g ground coriander, 5g turmeric powder, 5g garam masala, salt, pepper
- UK: 8 sheets phyllo pastry, 200g potatoes (peeled and diced), 100g carrots (peeled and diced), 1 onion (chopped), 2 cloves garlic (minced), 15ml olive oil, 5g ground cumin, 5g ground coriander, 5g turmeric powder, 5g garam masala, salt, pepper

Instructions:
1. Preheat your air fryer to 180°C (360°F).
2. In a large pan, heat olive oil over medium heat.
3. Add chopped onion and minced garlic, sauté until soft.
4. Stir in diced potatoes and carrots, cook until tender.
5. Add ground cumin, ground coriander, turmeric powder, garam masala, salt, and pepper, mix well.
6. Remove from heat and let the vegetable mixture cool slightly.
7. Cut each phyllo pastry sheet into 3 equal strips.
8. Place a spoonful of the vegetable mixture at one end of each strip.
9. Fold the pastry over the filling to form a triangle, continue folding until the end of the strip.
10. Brush the samosas with olive oil.
11. Arrange the samosas in the air fryer basket.
12. Air fry for 15-20 minutes until golden brown and crispy.
13. Serve the baked vegetable samosas hot with mango chutney or mint yogurt sauce!

Nutritional Info (per serving): Calories: 240 | Fat: 6g | Carbs: 42g | Protein: 5g

Air-Fried Jalapeño Poppers

Prep: 20 mins | Cook: 10 mins | Serves: 4

Ingredients:
- US: 8 jalapeño peppers, 100g cream cheese, 50g cheddar cheese (grated), 30g breadcrumbs, 5g garlic powder, 5g onion powder, salt, pepper
- UK: 8 jalapeño peppers, 100g cream cheese, 50g cheddar cheese (grated), 30g breadcrumbs, 5g garlic powder, 5g onion powder, salt, pepper

Instructions:
1. Preheat your air fryer to 180°C (360°F).
2. Cut the jalapeño peppers in half lengthwise and remove the seeds and membranes.
3. In a bowl, mix together cream cheese, grated cheddar cheese, breadcrumbs, garlic powder, onion powder, salt, and pepper until well combined.
4. Spoon the cheese mixture into the jalapeño halves, pressing gently to fill.
5. Arrange the stuffed jalapeños in the air fryer basket.
6. Air fry for 8-10 minutes until the jalapeños are tender and the cheese is melted and bubbly.
7. Serve the air-fried jalapeño poppers hot as a spicy and cheesy appetizer!

Nutritional Info (per serving): Calories: 160 | Fat: 10g | Carbs: 10g | Protein: 7g

Zucchini Fritters with Tzatziki Dip

Prep: 20 mins | Cook: 15 mins | Serves: 4

Ingredients:
- US: 2 medium zucchinis, 1 egg, 30g breadcrumbs, 30g grated Parmesan cheese, 1 clove garlic (minced), 15ml olive oil, salt, pepper
- UK: 2 medium zucchinis, 1 egg, 30g breadcrumbs, 30g grated Parmesan cheese, 1 clove garlic (minced), 15ml olive oil, salt, pepper

Instructions:
1. Grate the zucchinis and place them in a clean kitchen towel.
2. Squeeze out excess moisture from the grated zucchinis.
3. In a bowl, combine the grated zucchinis, egg, breadcrumbs, grated Parmesan cheese, minced garlic, salt, and pepper.
4. Heat olive oil in a frying pan over medium heat.
5. Spoon the zucchini mixture into the pan, forming small fritters.
6. Cook for 3-4 minutes on each side until golden brown and crispy.
7. Preheat your air fryer to 180°C (360°F).
8. Transfer the cooked fritters to the air fryer basket.
9. Air fry for 5-6 minutes to ensure they are heated through and extra crispy.
10. Serve the zucchini fritters hot with tzatziki dip for a refreshing contrast!

Nutritional Info (per serving): Calories: 120 | Fat: 7g | Carbs: 9g | Protein: 5g

Roasted Red Pepper Hummus with Veggie Sticks

Prep: 15 mins | Cook: 30 mins | Serves: 4

Ingredients:
- US: 1 can (400g) chickpeas, 1 large red bell pepper, 30ml olive oil, 1 clove garlic (minced), 30ml lemon juice, 5g ground cumin, salt, pepper, assorted vegetable sticks (carrots, cucumber, bell pepper) for serving
- UK: 1 can (400g) chickpeas, 1 large red bell pepper, 30ml olive oil, 1 clove garlic (minced), 30ml lemon juice, 5g ground cumin, salt, pepper, assorted vegetable sticks (carrots, cucumber, bell pepper) for serving

Instructions:
1. Preheat your air fryer to 200°C (400°F).
2. Cut the red bell pepper into large chunks, removing the seeds and membranes.
3. Toss the bell pepper chunks with olive oil, minced garlic, salt, and pepper until coated.
4. Arrange the seasoned bell pepper chunks in the air fryer basket.
5. Air fry for 25-30 minutes until the peppers are charred and tender.
6. In a food processor, combine the roasted red peppers, chickpeas, lemon juice, ground cumin, salt, and pepper.
7. Blend until smooth, adding a splash of water if needed to reach your desired consistency.
8. Serve the roasted red pepper hummus with assorted vegetable sticks for a nutritious and flavorful snack!

Nutritional Info (per serving): Calories: 180 | Fat: 9g | Carbs: 20g | Protein: 6g

Air-Fried Veggie Meatballs

Prep: 20 mins | Cook: 20 mins | Serves: 4

Ingredients:
- US: 200g mixed vegetables (carrots, peas, corn), 100g cooked quinoa, 30g breadcrumbs, 1 egg, 1 clove garlic (minced), 15ml olive oil, salt, pepper
- UK: 200g mixed vegetables (carrots, peas, corn), 100g cooked quinoa, 30g breadcrumbs, 1 egg, 1 clove garlic (minced), 15ml olive oil, salt, pepper

Instructions:
1. Preheat your air fryer to 180°C (360°F).
2. In a food processor, pulse the mixed vegetables until finely chopped.
3. In a large bowl, combine the chopped vegetables, cooked quinoa, breadcrumbs, egg, minced garlic, salt, and pepper.
4. Mix until well combined, then shape the mixture into small meatballs.
5. Lightly coat the veggie meatballs with olive oil.
6. Arrange the veggie meatballs in the air fryer basket.
7. Air fry for 15-20 minutes until golden brown and cooked through, turning halfway through.
8. Serve the air-fried veggie meatballs hot with marinara sauce for dipping or with pasta for a hearty meal!

Nutritional Info (per serving): Calories: 150 | Fat: 6g | Carbs: 20g | Protein: 6g

CHAPTER 3: SALADS AND SIDES

Air-Fried Brussels Sprouts with Balsamic Glaze
Prep: 10 mins | Cook: 15 mins | Serves: 4
Ingredients:
- US: 500g Brussels sprouts (trimmed and halved), 30ml olive oil, salt, pepper, 60ml balsamic glaze
- UK: 500g Brussels sprouts (trimmed and halved), 30ml olive oil, salt, pepper, 60ml balsamic glaze

Instructions:
1. Preheat your air fryer to 200°C (400°F).
2. In a bowl, toss Brussels sprouts with olive oil, salt, and pepper.
3. Arrange Brussels sprouts in the air fryer basket in a single layer.
4. Air fry for 12-15 minutes until crispy and browned.
5. Drizzle with balsamic glaze before serving.

Nutritional Info (per serving): Calories: 120 | Fat: 7g | Carbs: 14g | Protein: 4g

Roasted Cauliflower with Tahini Dressing
Prep: 10 mins | Cook: 20 mins | Serves: 4
Ingredients:
- US: 1 large cauliflower (cut into florets), 30ml olive oil, salt, pepper, 60ml tahini, 30ml lemon juice, 1 garlic clove (minced), water
- UK: 1 large cauliflower (cut into florets), 30ml olive oil, salt, pepper, 60ml tahini, 30ml lemon juice, 1 garlic clove (minced), water

Instructions:
1. Preheat your air fryer to 200°C (400°F).
2. In a bowl, toss cauliflower florets with olive oil, salt, and pepper.
3. Arrange cauliflower in the air fryer basket in a single layer.
4. Air fry for 18-20 minutes until golden brown and tender.
5. In a small bowl, whisk together tahini, lemon juice, minced garlic, and enough water to thin the dressing.
6. Drizzle roasted cauliflower with tahini dressing before serving.

Nutritional Info (per serving): Calories: 180 | Fat: 12g | Carbs: 15g | Protein: 6g

Grilled Vegetable Salad with Balsamic Vinaigrette
Prep: 15 mins | Cook: 10 mins | Serves: 4
Ingredients:
- US: 1 zucchini (sliced), 1 yellow squash (sliced), 1 red bell pepper (sliced), 1 red onion (sliced), 30ml olive oil, salt, pepper, 60ml balsamic vinegar, 30ml olive oil, 1 garlic clove (minced), 1 teaspoon Dijon mustard
- UK: 1 zucchini (sliced), 1 yellow squash (sliced), 1 red bell pepper (sliced), 1 red onion (sliced), 30ml olive oil, salt, pepper, 60ml balsamic vinegar, 30ml olive oil, 1 garlic clove (minced), 1 teaspoon Dijon mustard

Instructions:
1. Preheat your air fryer to 200°C (400°F).
2. In a bowl, toss zucchini, yellow squash, bell pepper, and red onion with olive oil, salt, and pepper.
3. Arrange vegetables in the air fryer basket in a single layer.
4. Air fry for 8-10 minutes until vegetables are tender and slightly charred.
5. In a small bowl, whisk together balsamic vinegar, olive oil, minced garlic, and Dijon mustard to make the vinaigrette.

6. Transfer grilled vegetables to a serving platter and drizzle with balsamic vinaigrette before serving.

Nutritional Info (per serving): Calories: 150 | Fat: 10g | Carbs: 12g | Protein: 3g

Air-Fried Sweet Potato Fries

Prep: 10 mins | Cook: 20 mins | Serves: 4

Ingredients:
- US: 2 large sweet potatoes (cut into fries), 30ml olive oil, 1 teaspoon paprika, 1/2 teaspoon garlic powder, salt, pepper
- UK: 2 large sweet potatoes (cut into fries), 30ml olive oil, 1 teaspoon paprika, 1/2 teaspoon garlic powder, salt, pepper

Instructions:
1. Preheat your air fryer to 200°C (400°F).
2. In a bowl, toss sweet potato fries with olive oil, paprika, garlic powder, salt, and pepper.
3. Arrange fries in the air fryer basket in a single layer.
4. Air fry for 18-20 minutes until crispy and golden brown.
5. Serve hot with your favorite dipping sauce.

Nutritional Info (per serving): Calories: 150 | Fat: 7g | Carbs: 20g | Protein: 2g

Baked Stuffed Tomatoes

Prep: 15 mins | Cook: 25 mins | Serves: 4

Ingredients:
- US: 4 large tomatoes, 100g cooked quinoa, 1/2 red onion (diced), 1/2 red bell pepper (diced), 50g feta cheese (crumbled), 2 tablespoons chopped fresh parsley, salt, pepper, olive oil
- UK: 4 large tomatoes, 100g cooked quinoa, 1/2 red onion (diced), 1/2 red bell pepper (diced), 50g feta cheese (crumbled), 2 tablespoons chopped fresh parsley, salt, pepper, olive oil

Instructions:
1. Preheat your oven to 200°C (400°F).
2. Cut the tops off the tomatoes and scoop out the seeds and pulp.
3. In a bowl, mix together cooked quinoa, diced red onion, diced red bell pepper, crumbled feta cheese, chopped parsley, salt, and pepper.
4. Stuff each tomato with the quinoa mixture.
5. Place stuffed tomatoes on a baking dish.
6. Drizzle with olive oil.
7. Bake for 20-25 minutes until tomatoes are softened and tops are golden brown.
8. Serve hot.

Nutritional Info (per serving): Calories: 120 | Fat: 5g | Carbs: 15g | Protein: 4g

Air-Fried Vegetable Skewers

Prep: 15 mins | Cook: 15 mins | Serves: 4

Ingredients:
- US: 1 zucchini (sliced), 1 yellow squash (sliced), 1 red bell pepper (diced), 1 red onion (quartered), cherry tomatoes, 30ml olive oil, salt, pepper, wooden skewers (soaked in water)
- UK: 1 zucchini (sliced), 1 yellow squash (sliced), 1 red bell pepper (diced), 1 red onion (quartered), cherry tomatoes, 30ml olive oil, salt, pepper, wooden skewers (soaked in water)

Instructions:
1. Preheat your air fryer to 200°C (400°F).
2. Thread zucchini, yellow squash, red bell pepper, red onion, and cherry tomatoes onto skewers.

3. Brush vegetable skewers with olive oil and season with salt and pepper.
4. Arrange skewers in the air fryer basket.
5. Air fry for 12-15 minutes until vegetables are tender and slightly charred.
6. Serve hot as a side dish or appetizer.

Nutritional Info (per serving): Calories: 100 | Fat: 7g | Carbs: 10g | Protein: 2g

Roasted Beet and Arugula Salad

Prep: 15 mins | Cook: 45 mins | Serves: 4

Ingredients:
- US: 4 medium beets (peeled and diced), 30ml olive oil, salt, pepper, 120g arugula, 60g goat cheese (crumbled), 30g walnuts (toasted), balsamic vinegar
- UK: 4 medium beets (peeled and diced), 30ml olive oil, salt, pepper, 120g arugula, 60g goat cheese (crumbled), 30g walnuts (toasted), balsamic vinegar

Instructions:
1. Preheat your oven to 200°C (400°F).
2. Toss diced beets with olive oil, salt, and pepper.
3. Spread beets in a single layer on a baking sheet.
4. Roast for 40-45 minutes until tender.
5. In a large bowl, combine roasted beets, arugula, crumbled goat cheese, and toasted walnuts.
6. Drizzle with balsamic vinegar before serving.

Nutritional Info (per serving): Calories: 200 | Fat: 12g | Carbs: 15g | Protein: 7g

Crispy Air-Fried Kale Chips

Prep: 5 mins | Cook: 10 mins | Serves: 4

Ingredients:
- US: 1 bunch kale (stems removed and torn into bite-sized pieces), 15ml olive oil, salt, pepper, nutritional yeast (optional)
- UK: 1 bunch kale (stems removed and torn into bite-sized pieces), 15ml olive oil, salt, pepper, nutritional yeast (optional)

Instructions:
1. Preheat your air fryer to 160°C (325°F).
2. In a bowl, massage kale pieces with olive oil, salt, and pepper until evenly coated.
3. Arrange kale in the air fryer basket in a single layer.
4. Air fry for 8-10 minutes until crispy, shaking the basket halfway through.
5. Sprinkle with nutritional yeast, if desired, before serving.

Nutritional Info (per serving): Calories: 50 | Fat: 3g | Carbs: 5g | Protein: 2g

Grilled Corn on the Cob with Herb Butter

Prep: 10 mins | Cook: 15 mins | Serves: 4

Ingredients:
- US: 4 ears corn on the cob (husks removed), 60g butter (softened), 2 tablespoons chopped fresh herbs (parsley, chives, thyme), salt, pepper
- UK: 4 ears corn on the cob (husks removed), 60g butter (softened), 2 tablespoons chopped fresh herbs (parsley, chives, thyme), salt, pepper

Instructions:
1. Preheat your grill to medium heat.
2. In a bowl, mix together softened butter, chopped fresh herbs, salt, and pepper.
3. Rub herb butter over each ear of corn.
4. Grill corn on the cob for 10-15 minutes, turning occasionally, until charred and tender.
5. Serve hot.

Nutritional Info (per serving): Calories: 180 | Fat: 10g | Carbs: 20g | Protein: 4g

Roasted Butternut Squash with Cranberries and Pecans

Prep: 15 mins | Cook: 30 mins | Serves: 4

Ingredients:
- US: 1 medium butternut squash (peeled, seeded, and diced), 30ml olive oil, salt, pepper, 60g dried cranberries, 30g chopped pecans, 1 tablespoon maple syrup
- UK: 1 medium butternut squash (peeled, seeded, and diced), 30ml olive oil, salt, pepper, 60g dried cranberries, 30g chopped pecans, 1 tablespoon maple syrup

Instructions:
1. Preheat your oven to 200°C (400°F).
2. In a bowl, toss diced butternut squash with olive oil, salt, and pepper.
3. Spread butternut squash on a baking sheet in a single layer.
4. Roast for 25-30 minutes until tender and caramelized.
5. In a small bowl, mix together dried cranberries, chopped pecans, and maple syrup.
6. Remove roasted butternut squash from the oven and sprinkle with cranberry-pecan mixture.
7. Return to the oven and roast for an additional 5 minutes.
8. Serve hot as a side dish.

Nutritional Info (per serving): Calories: 200 | Fat: 10g | Carbs: 25g | Protein: 2g

CHAPTER 4: SANDWICHES AND WRAPS

Air-Fried Falafel Wraps with Tahini Sauce
Prep: 20 mins | Cook: 15 mins | Serves: 4
Ingredients:
- US: 8 falafel balls, 4 whole wheat wraps, 100g lettuce leaves, 1 tomato (sliced), 1/2 cucumber (sliced), 60ml tahini sauce
- UK: 8 falafel balls, 4 whole wheat wraps, 100g lettuce leaves, 1 tomato (sliced), 1/2 cucumber (sliced), 60ml tahini sauce

Instructions:
1. Preheat your air fryer to 180°C (360°F).
2. Place the falafel balls in the air fryer basket.
3. Air fry for 12-15 minutes until crispy and heated through.
4. Warm the whole wheat wraps in a dry skillet or microwave.
5. Place lettuce leaves, sliced tomato, sliced cucumber, and air-fried falafel in the center of each wrap.
6. Drizzle with tahini sauce.
7. Fold in the sides of the wraps and roll tightly.
8. Serve the falafel wraps immediately for a delicious and satisfying meal!

Nutritional Info (per serving): Calories: 350 | Fat: 12g | Carbs: 50g | Protein: 14g

Veggie Panini with Pesto and Roasted Peppers
Prep: 15 mins | Cook: 10 mins | Serves: 2
Ingredients:
- US: 4 slices ciabatta bread, 60g pesto sauce, 100g roasted bell peppers (sliced), 1 small zucchini (sliced), 1 small red onion (sliced), 60g mozzarella cheese (sliced), 15ml olive oil
- UK: 4 slices ciabatta bread, 60g pesto sauce, 100g roasted bell peppers (sliced), 1 small zucchini (sliced), 1 small red onion (sliced), 60g mozzarella cheese (sliced), 15ml olive oil

Instructions:
1. Preheat your panini press.
2. Brush one side of each slice of ciabatta bread with olive oil.
3. Spread pesto sauce on the other side of each slice.
4. Layer roasted bell peppers, sliced zucchini, sliced red onion, and mozzarella cheese on two slices of bread.
5. Top with the remaining slices of bread, oiled side up.
6. Place the sandwiches in the panini press and cook for 5-7 minutes until golden brown and the cheese is melted.
7. Slice the panini in half and serve hot with a side salad for a delicious and satisfying meal!

Nutritional Info (per serving): Calories: 450 | Fat: 20g | Carbs: 50g | Protein: 16g

Tofu Banh Mi with Quick Pickled Veggies

Prep: 30 mins | Cook: 15 mins | Serves: 4

Ingredients:
- US: 200g firm tofu, 4 baguettes, 100g pickled daikon and carrot, 1 cucumber (sliced), 60ml vegan mayonnaise, 15ml soy sauce, 15ml rice vinegar, 5ml sesame oil, salt, pepper, fresh cilantro (for garnish)
- UK: 200g firm tofu, 4 baguettes, 100g pickled daikon and carrot, 1 cucumber (sliced), 60ml vegan mayonnaise, 15ml soy sauce, 15ml rice vinegar, 5ml sesame oil, salt, pepper, fresh cilantro (for garnish)

Instructions:
1. Press the tofu to remove excess moisture, then slice into 1/2-inch thick pieces.
2. In a small bowl, whisk together soy sauce, rice vinegar, sesame oil, salt, and pepper.
3. Marinate the tofu slices in the mixture for at least 20 minutes.
4. Preheat your air fryer to 200°C (400°F).
5. Air fry the marinated tofu slices for 12-15 minutes until golden and crispy.
6. Slice the baguettes lengthwise, then spread vegan mayonnaise on one side.
7. Layer tofu slices, pickled daikon and carrot, and sliced cucumber on the baguettes.
8. Garnish with fresh cilantro.
9. Serve the tofu Banh Mi sandwiches with extra pickled veggies on the side for a burst of flavor!

Nutritional Info (per serving): Calories: 380 | Fat: 12g | Carbs: 52g | Protein: 15g

Grilled Vegetable and Hummus Wraps

Prep: 20 mins | Cook: 15 mins | Serves: 4

Ingredients:
- US: 4 large tortilla wraps, 200g mixed grilled vegetables (zucchini, bell peppers, eggplant), 200g hummus, 100g spinach leaves, 1 avocado (sliced), salt, pepper
- UK: 4 large tortilla wraps, 200g mixed grilled vegetables (zucchini, bell peppers, eggplant), 200g hummus, 100g spinach leaves, 1 avocado (sliced), salt, pepper

Instructions:
1. Warm the tortilla wraps in a dry skillet or microwave.
2. Spread a generous amount of hummus onto each wrap.
3. Layer grilled vegetables, spinach leaves, and sliced avocado on top of the hummus.
4. Season with salt and pepper to taste.
5. Fold in the sides of the wraps and roll tightly.
6. Slice the wraps in half and serve immediately for a wholesome and flavorful lunch!

Nutritional Info (per serving): Calories: 320 | Fat: 15g | Carbs: 40g | Protein: 10g

Air-Fried Portobello Mushroom Burgers

Prep: 20 mins | Cook: 15 mins | Serves: 4

Ingredients:
- US: 4 large portobello mushrooms, 4 burger buns, 100g baby spinach leaves, 1 tomato (sliced), 1 red onion (sliced), 60g vegan cheese slices, 15ml balsamic vinegar, 15ml olive oil, salt, pepper
- UK: 4 large portobello mushrooms, 4 burger buns, 100g baby spinach leaves, 1 tomato (sliced), 1 red onion (sliced), 60g vegan cheese slices, 15ml balsamic vinegar, 15ml olive oil, salt, pepper

Instructions:
1. Preheat your air fryer to 200°C (400°F).
2. Remove the stems from the portobello mushrooms and brush both sides with olive oil and balsamic vinegar.
3. Season with salt and pepper to taste.

4. Place the mushrooms in the air fryer basket.
5. Air fry for 12-15 minutes until tender and juicy.
6. Assemble the mushroom burgers by placing a mushroom on each burger bun.
7. Top with baby spinach leaves, sliced tomato, sliced red onion, and vegan cheese slices.
8. Serve the air-fried portobello mushroom burgers hot with your favorite condiments for a satisfying meat-free meal!

Nutritional Info (per serving): Calories: 280 | Fat: 10g | Carbs: 40g | Protein: 10g

Crispy Tofu Sandwiches with Sriracha Mayo

Prep: 30 mins | Cook: 15 mins | Serves: 4

Ingredients:
- US: 200g firm tofu, 4 sandwich rolls, 100g mixed salad greens, 60ml vegan mayonnaise, 15ml sriracha sauce, 15ml soy sauce, 5ml maple syrup, 5ml sesame oil, salt, pepper
- UK: 200g firm tofu, 4 sandwich rolls, 100g mixed salad greens, 60ml vegan mayonnaise, 15ml sriracha sauce, 15ml soy sauce, 5ml maple syrup, 5ml sesame oil, salt, pepper

Instructions:
1. Press the tofu to remove excess moisture, then slice into 1/2-inch thick pieces.
2. In a small bowl, whisk together soy sauce, maple syrup, sesame oil, salt, and pepper.
3. Marinate the tofu slices in the mixture for at least 20 minutes.
4. Preheat your air fryer to 200°C (400°F).
5. Air fry the marinated tofu slices for 12-15 minutes until crispy.
6. In a separate bowl, mix together vegan mayonnaise and sriracha sauce to make the spicy mayo.
7. Slice the sandwich rolls and spread spicy mayo on one side of each roll.
8. Layer crispy tofu slices and mixed salad greens on the rolls.
9. Serve the crispy tofu sandwiches immediately with extra sriracha mayo on the side for an extra kick!

Nutritional Info (per serving): Calories: 320 | Fat: 15g | Carbs: 35g | Protein: 15g

Mediterranean Veggie Pitas

Prep: 20 mins | Cook: 10 mins | Serves: 4

Ingredients:
- US: 4 whole wheat pita bread, 200g mixed salad greens, 1 cucumber (sliced), 1 bell pepper (sliced), 1 tomato (sliced), 1/2 red onion (sliced), 100g feta cheese (crumbled), 60ml Greek dressing
- UK: 4 whole wheat pita bread, 200g mixed salad greens, 1 cucumber (sliced), 1 bell pepper (sliced), 1 tomato (sliced), 1/2 red onion (sliced), 100g feta cheese (crumbled), 60ml Greek dressing

Instructions:
1. Cut the whole wheat pita bread in half to form pockets.
2. Fill each pita pocket with mixed salad greens, sliced cucumber, bell pepper, tomato, and red onion.
3. Sprinkle crumbled feta cheese over the veggies.
4. Drizzle Greek dressing inside each pita pocket.
5. Serve the Mediterranean veggie pitas immediately for a refreshing and satisfying lunch!

Nutritional Info (per serving): Calories: 280 | Fat: 10g | Carbs: 35g | Protein: 12g

Air-Fried Eggplant Parmesan Sandwiches

Prep: 30 mins | Cook: 20 mins | Serves: 4

Ingredients:
- ❖ US: 1 large eggplant, 4 sandwich rolls, 200g marinara sauce, 100g mozzarella cheese (sliced), 30g grated Parmesan cheese, 30g breadcrumbs, 15ml olive oil, salt, pepper
- ❖ UK: 1 large eggplant, 4 sandwich rolls, 200g marinara sauce, 100g mozzarella cheese (sliced), 30g grated Parmesan cheese, 30g breadcrumbs, 15ml olive oil, salt, pepper

Instructions:
1. Preheat your air fryer to 180°C (360°F).
2. Slice the eggplant into 1/2-inch thick rounds.
3. In a shallow dish, mix together breadcrumbs, grated Parmesan cheese, salt, and pepper.
4. Dip each eggplant slice into the breadcrumb mixture, pressing gently to coat.
5. Place the breaded eggplant slices in the air fryer basket.
6. Air fry for 15-20 minutes until golden brown and crispy.
7. Slice the sandwich rolls and lightly toast them.
8. Spread marinara sauce on one side of each roll.
9. Layer air-fried eggplant slices and sliced mozzarella cheese on top of the sauce.
10. Close the sandwiches and press gently.
11. Serve the air-fried eggplant Parmesan sandwiches hot with a side salad for a comforting and flavorful meal!

Nutritional Info (per serving): Calories: 350 | Fat: 15g | Carbs: 40g | Protein: 15g

Vegan BLT Wraps with Tempeh Bacon

Prep: 30 mins | Cook: 15 mins | Serves: 4

Ingredients:
- ❖ US: 200g tempeh, 4 whole grain wraps, 100g lettuce leaves, 2 tomatoes (sliced), 60ml vegan mayonnaise, 30ml maple syrup, 15ml soy sauce, 15ml olive oil, salt, pepper
- ❖ UK: 200g tempeh, 4 whole grain wraps, 100g lettuce leaves, 2 tomatoes (sliced), 60ml vegan mayonnaise, 30ml maple syrup, 15ml soy sauce, 15ml olive oil, salt, pepper

Instructions:
1. Slice the tempeh into thin strips.
2. In a small bowl, whisk together maple syrup, soy sauce, olive oil, salt, and pepper.
3. Marinate the tempeh strips in the mixture for at least 20 minutes.
4. Preheat your air fryer to 180°C (360°F).
5. Air fry the marinated tempeh strips for 12-15 minutes until crispy.
6. Warm the whole grain wraps in a dry skillet or microwave.
7. Spread vegan mayonnaise on one side of each wrap.
8. Layer lettuce leaves, sliced tomatoes, and crispy tempeh strips on top of the mayonnaise.
9. Roll up the wraps tightly and slice in half.
10. Serve the vegan BLT wraps immediately for a delicious and satisfying meal!

Nutritional Info (per serving): Calories: 320 | Fat: 15g | Carbs: 35g | Protein: 15g

Roasted Vegetable and Pesto Panini

Prep: 20 mins | Cook: 15 mins | Serves: 2

Ingredients:
- US: 4 slices sourdough bread, 60g pesto sauce, 100g roasted vegetables (zucchini, bell peppers, red onion), 60g mozzarella cheese (sliced), 15ml olive oil
- UK: 4 slices sourdough bread, 60g pesto sauce, 100g roasted vegetables (zucchini, bell peppers, red onion), 60g mozzarella cheese (sliced), 15ml olive oil

Instructions:
1. Preheat your panini press.
2. Brush one side of each slice of sourdough bread with olive oil.
3. Spread pesto sauce on the other side of each slice.
4. Layer roasted vegetables and mozzarella cheese on two slices of bread.
5. Top with the remaining slices of bread, oiled side up.
6. Place the sandwiches in the panini press and cook for 5-7 minutes until golden brown and the cheese is melted.
7. Slice the panini in half and serve hot with a side salad for a delicious and satisfying meal!

Nutritional Info (per serving): Calories: 400 | Fat: 20g | Carbs: 45g | Protein: 15g

CHAPTER 5: SOUPS AND STEWS

Roasted Vegetable Soup with Air-Fried Croutons
Prep: 15 mins | Cook: 45 mins | Serves: 4
Ingredients:
- US: 2 large carrots (chopped), 2 stalks celery (chopped), 1 onion (chopped), 2 bell peppers (chopped), 3 tomatoes (quartered), 4 cloves garlic (minced), 30ml olive oil, salt, pepper, 1 liter vegetable broth, 4 slices whole grain bread (cubed)
- UK: 2 large carrots (chopped), 2 stalks celery (chopped), 1 onion (chopped), 2 bell peppers (chopped), 3 tomatoes (quartered), 4 cloves garlic (minced), 30ml olive oil, salt, pepper, 1 liter vegetable broth, 4 slices whole grain bread (cubed)

Instructions:
1. Preheat your oven to 200°C (400°F).
2. In a large bowl, toss carrots, celery, onion, bell peppers, tomatoes, and minced garlic with olive oil, salt, and pepper.
3. Spread vegetables on a baking sheet in a single layer.
4. Roast for 40-45 minutes until vegetables are caramelized.
5. Transfer roasted vegetables to a pot and add vegetable broth.
6. Bring to a simmer and cook for 10-15 minutes.
7. Meanwhile, preheat your air fryer to 180°C (350°F).
8. Toss bread cubes with a little olive oil, salt, and pepper.
9. Air fry bread cubes for 5-7 minutes until golden and crispy.
10. Serve roasted vegetable soup with air-fried croutons on top.

Nutritional Info (per serving): Calories: 250 | Fat: 10g | Carbs: 35g | Protein: 5g

Lentil and Sweet Potato Stew
Prep: 15 mins | Cook: 30 mins | Serves: 4
Ingredients:
- US: 200g dry lentils, 2 sweet potatoes (peeled and diced), 1 onion (chopped), 2 carrots (chopped), 2 celery stalks (chopped), 4 cups vegetable broth, 2 teaspoons curry powder, salt, pepper, fresh parsley (for garnish)
- UK: 200g dry lentils, 2 sweet potatoes (peeled and diced), 1 onion (chopped), 2 carrots (chopped), 2 celery stalks (chopped), 4 cups vegetable broth, 2 teaspoons curry powder, salt, pepper, fresh parsley (for garnish)

Instructions:
1. Rinse lentils under cold water.
2. In a large pot, combine lentils, sweet potatoes, onion, carrots, celery, vegetable broth, curry powder, salt, and pepper.
3. Bring to a boil, then reduce heat and simmer for 25-30 minutes until lentils and sweet potatoes are tender.
4. Season with additional salt and pepper if needed.
5. Ladle stew into bowls and garnish with fresh parsley before serving.

Nutritional Info (per serving): Calories: 300 | Fat: 1g | Carbs: 60g | Protein: 18g

Creamy Tomato Soup with Air-Fried Basil Croutons

Prep: 10 mins | Cook: 25 mins | Serves: 4

Ingredients:
- US: 2 tablespoons olive oil, 1 onion (chopped), 2 cloves garlic (minced), 800g canned tomatoes, 2 cups vegetable broth, 120ml coconut milk, salt, pepper, fresh basil leaves, 4 slices whole grain bread (cubed)
- UK: 2 tablespoons olive oil, 1 onion (chopped), 2 cloves garlic (minced), 800g canned tomatoes, 2 cups vegetable broth, 120ml coconut milk, salt, pepper, fresh basil leaves, 4 slices whole grain bread (cubed)

Instructions:
1. In a large pot, heat olive oil over medium heat.
2. Add chopped onion and minced garlic, and sauté until softened.
3. Stir in canned tomatoes (with juices) and vegetable broth.
4. Bring to a simmer and cook for 15-20 minutes.
5. Use an immersion blender to puree the soup until smooth.
6. Stir in coconut milk and season with salt and pepper to taste.
7. Meanwhile, preheat your air fryer to 180°C (350°F).
8. Toss bread cubes with a little olive oil and fresh basil leaves.
9. Air fry bread cubes for 5-7 minutes until golden and crispy.
10. Serve creamy tomato soup with air-fried basil croutons on top.

Nutritional Info (per serving): Calories: 250 | Fat: 10g | Carbs: 35g | Protein: 5g

Vegan Chili with Air-Fried Tortilla Strips

Prep: 15 mins | Cook: 45 mins | Serves: 4

Ingredients:
- US: 1 onion (chopped), 2 cloves garlic (minced), 1 red bell pepper (chopped), 1 green bell pepper (chopped), 2 carrots (chopped), 400g canned kidney beans (drained and rinsed), 400g canned black beans (drained and rinsed), 800g canned diced tomatoes, 2 cups vegetable broth, 2 teaspoons chili powder, 1 teaspoon cumin, salt, pepper, 4 corn tortillas (cut into strips)
- UK: 1 onion (chopped), 2 cloves garlic (minced), 1 red bell pepper (chopped), 1 green bell pepper (chopped), 2 carrots (chopped), 400g canned kidney beans (drained and rinsed), 400g canned black beans (drained and rinsed), 800g canned diced tomatoes, 2 cups vegetable broth, 2 teaspoons chili powder, 1 teaspoon cumin, salt, pepper, 4 corn tortillas (cut into strips)

Instructions:
1. In a large pot, sauté chopped onion and minced garlic until softened.
2. Add chopped bell peppers and carrots, and cook until slightly softened.
3. Stir in drained and rinsed kidney beans, black beans, diced tomatoes, vegetable broth, chili powder, cumin, salt, and pepper.
4. Bring to a simmer and cook for 30-40 minutes.
5. Meanwhile, preheat your air fryer to 180°C (350°F).
6. Toss tortilla strips with a little olive oil, chili powder, cumin, salt, and pepper.
7. Air fry tortilla strips for 5-7 minutes until crispy.
8. Serve vegan chili with air-fried tortilla strips on top.

Nutritional Info (per serving): Calories: 300 | Fat: 5g | Carbs: 50g | Protein: 15g

Curried Cauliflower Soup

Prep: 10 mins | Cook: 30 mins | Serves: 4

Ingredients:
- US: 1 head cauliflower (cut into florets), 1 onion (chopped), 2 cloves garlic (minced), 1 tablespoon curry powder, 1 teaspoon ground cumin, 1/2 teaspoon ground turmeric, 4 cups vegetable broth, 120ml coconut milk, salt, pepper, fresh cilantro (for garnish)
- UK: 1 head cauliflower (cut into florets), 1 onion (chopped), 2 cloves garlic (minced), 1 tablespoon curry powder, 1 teaspoon ground cumin, 1/2 teaspoon ground turmeric, 4 cups vegetable broth, 120ml coconut milk, salt, pepper, fresh cilantro (for garnish)

Instructions:
1. In a large pot, sauté chopped onion and minced garlic until softened.
2. Add cauliflower florets, curry powder, ground cumin, and ground turmeric, and cook for 2-3 minutes.
3. Stir in vegetable broth and bring to a simmer.
4. Cook for 20-25 minutes until cauliflower is tender.
5. Use an immersion blender to puree the soup until smooth.
6. Stir in coconut milk and season with salt and pepper to taste.
7. Ladle soup into bowls and garnish with fresh cilantro before serving.

Nutritional Info (per serving): Calories: 200 | Fat: 10g | Carbs: 25g | Protein: 5g

Italian Vegetable Minestrone

Prep: 15 mins | Cook: 45 mins | Serves: 4

Ingredients:
- US: 1 onion (chopped), 2 cloves garlic (minced), 2 carrots (chopped), 2 stalks celery (chopped), 1 zucchini (chopped), 1 yellow squash (chopped), 1 bell pepper (chopped), 400g canned diced tomatoes, 4 cups vegetable broth, 100g small pasta, 400g canned cannellini beans (drained and rinsed), 1 teaspoon dried oregano, 1 teaspoon dried basil, salt, pepper, fresh parsley (for garnish)
- UK: 1 onion (chopped), 2 cloves garlic (minced), 2 carrots (chopped), 2 stalks celery (chopped), 1 zucchini (chopped), 1 yellow squash (chopped), 1 bell pepper (chopped), 400g canned diced tomatoes, 4 cups vegetable broth, 100g small pasta, 400g canned cannellini beans (drained and rinsed), 1 teaspoon dried oregano, 1 teaspoon dried basil, salt, pepper, fresh parsley (for garnish)

Instructions:
1. In a large pot, sauté chopped onion and minced garlic until softened.
2. Add chopped carrots, celery, zucchini, yellow squash, and bell pepper, and cook for 5-7 minutes.
3. Stir in canned diced tomatoes, vegetable broth, small pasta, drained and rinsed cannellini beans, dried oregano, and dried basil.
4. Bring to a simmer and cook for 20-25 minutes until pasta is tender.
5. Season with salt and pepper to taste.
6. Ladle minestrone into bowls and garnish with fresh parsley before serving.

Nutritional Info (per serving): Calories: 300 | Fat: 2g | Carbs: 55g | Protein: 12g

Air-Fried Crispy Chickpeas for Soups and Salads

Prep: 5 mins | Cook: 20 mins | Serves: 4

Ingredients:
- ❖ US: 400g canned chickpeas (drained and rinsed), 15ml olive oil, 1 teaspoon smoked paprika, 1 teaspoon garlic powder, salt, pepper
- ❖ UK: 400g canned chickpeas (drained and rinsed), 15ml olive oil, 1 teaspoon smoked paprika, 1 teaspoon garlic powder, salt, pepper

Instructions:
1. Preheat your air fryer to 200°C (400°F).
2. Pat chickpeas dry with paper towels to remove excess moisture.
3. In a bowl, toss chickpeas with olive oil, smoked paprika, garlic powder, salt, and pepper.
4. Spread chickpeas in a single layer in the air fryer basket.
5. Air fry for 15-20 minutes until crispy, shaking the basket halfway through.
6. Serve crispy chickpeas as a topping for soups or salads.

Nutritional Info (per serving): Calories: 150 | Fat: 5g | Carbs: 20g | Protein: 6g

Roasted Butternut Squash Soup

Prep: 15 mins | Cook: 45 mins | Serves: 4

Ingredients:
- ❖ US: 1 large butternut squash (peeled, seeded, and diced), 1 onion (chopped), 2 cloves garlic (minced), 30ml olive oil, 4 cups vegetable broth, salt, pepper, 60ml coconut cream, fresh thyme leaves (for garnish)
- ❖ UK: 1 large butternut squash (peeled, seeded, and diced), 1 onion (chopped), 2 cloves garlic (minced), 30ml olive oil, 4 cups vegetable broth, salt, pepper, 60ml coconut cream, fresh thyme leaves (for garnish)

Instructions:
1. Preheat your oven to 200°C (400°F).
2. In a large bowl, toss diced butternut squash, chopped onion, and minced garlic with olive oil, salt, and pepper.
3. Spread mixture on a baking sheet in a single layer.
4. Roast for 40-45 minutes until squash is tender and caramelized.
5. Transfer roasted butternut squash, onion, and garlic to a pot.
6. Add vegetable broth and bring to a simmer.
7. Use an immersion blender to puree the soup until smooth.
8. Stir in coconut cream and season with salt and pepper to taste.
9. Ladle soup into bowls and garnish with fresh thyme leaves before serving.

Nutritional Info (per serving): Calories: 200 | Fat: 10g | Carbs: 25g | Protein: 2g

Vegetable Noodle Soup

Prep: 15 mins | Cook: 25 mins | Serves: 4

Ingredients:
- ❖ US: 4 cups vegetable broth, 2 carrots (sliced), 2 celery stalks (sliced), 1 onion (chopped), 2 cloves garlic (minced), 100g green beans (cut into pieces), 100g peas, 100g corn kernels, 100g egg noodles, salt, pepper, fresh parsley (for garnish)
- ❖ UK: 4 cups vegetable broth, 2 carrots (sliced), 2 celery stalks (sliced), 1 onion (chopped), 2 cloves garlic (minced), 100g green beans (cut into pieces), 100g peas, 100g corn kernels, 100g egg noodles, salt, pepper, fresh parsley (for garnish)

Instructions:
1. In a large pot, bring vegetable broth to a boil.
2. Add sliced carrots, celery, chopped onion, minced garlic, green beans, peas, and corn kernels.
3. Simmer for 15-20 minutes until vegetables are tender.
4. Stir in egg noodles and cook for an additional 5-7 minutes until noodles are cooked.
5. Season with salt and pepper to taste.
6. Ladle vegetable noodle soup into bowls and garnish with fresh parsley before serving.

Nutritional Info (per serving): Calories: 250 | Fat: 2g | Carbs: 45g | Protein: 8g

Air-Fried Veggie Meatballs for Stews

Prep: 15 mins | Cook: 20 mins | Serves: 4

Ingredients:
- US: 1 cup cooked quinoa, 200g cooked lentils, 1 carrot (grated), 1 zucchini (grated), 1 onion (finely chopped), 2 cloves garlic (minced), 30g breadcrumbs, 1 tablespoon tomato paste, 1 teaspoon dried oregano, 1 teaspoon dried basil, salt, pepper, olive oil spray
- UK: 1 cup cooked quinoa, 200g cooked lentils, 1 carrot (grated), 1 zucchini (grated), 1 onion (finely chopped), 2 cloves garlic (minced), 30g breadcrumbs, 1 tablespoon tomato paste, 1 teaspoon dried oregano, 1 teaspoon dried basil, salt, pepper, olive oil spray

Instructions:
1. Preheat your air fryer to 180°C (350°F).
2. In a large bowl, combine cooked quinoa, cooked lentils, grated carrot, grated zucchini, chopped onion, minced garlic, breadcrumbs, tomato paste, dried oregano, dried basil, salt, and pepper.
3. Use your hands to mix until well combined.
4. Shape mixture into small meatballs.
5. Lightly spray meatballs with olive oil spray.
6. Place meatballs in the air fryer basket in a single layer.
7. Air fry for 15-20 minutes until golden brown and cooked through.
8. Serve veggie meatballs in stews or with your favorite sauce.

Nutritional Info (per serving): Calories: 200 | Fat: 3g | Carbs: 30g | Protein: 10g

CHAPTER 6: VEGGIE MAINS

Air-Fried Tofu Steaks with Mushroom Gravy

Prep: 20 mins | Cook: 15 mins | Serves: 4

Ingredients:
- US: 400g firm tofu, 250g mushrooms (sliced), 2 cloves garlic (minced), 15ml soy sauce, 5ml Worcestershire sauce, 250ml vegetable broth, 30g all-purpose flour, 30ml olive oil, salt, pepper, fresh parsley (for garnish)
- UK: 400g firm tofu, 250g mushrooms (sliced), 2 cloves garlic (minced), 15ml soy sauce, 5ml Worcestershire sauce, 250ml vegetable broth, 30g all-purpose flour, 30ml olive oil, salt, pepper, fresh parsley (for garnish)

Instructions:
1. Press the tofu to remove excess moisture, then slice into thick steaks.
2. In a bowl, whisk together vegetable broth and all-purpose flour to make a slurry.
3. Preheat your air fryer to 200°C (400°F).
4. In a skillet, heat olive oil over medium heat.
5. Add minced garlic and sliced mushrooms, sauté until mushrooms are golden brown.
6. Pour in soy sauce and Worcestershire sauce, stir to combine.
7. Gradually add the slurry to the skillet, stirring constantly until the gravy thickens.
8. Place the tofu steaks in the air fryer basket.
9. Air fry for 10-12 minutes until golden and crispy.
10. Serve the air-fried tofu steaks with mushroom gravy, garnished with fresh parsley for a hearty and flavorful meal!

Nutritional Info (per serving): Calories: 250 | Fat: 12g | Carbs: 15g | Protein: 20g

Vegetable Fritters with Yogurt Sauce

Prep: 20 mins | Cook: 15 mins | Serves: 4

Ingredients:
- US: 2 large potatoes (grated), 2 carrots (grated), 1 zucchini (grated), 1 onion (finely chopped), 2 eggs, 60g all-purpose flour, 5ml baking powder, 5g paprika, salt, pepper, 120ml Greek yogurt, 15ml lemon juice, fresh dill (chopped, for garnish)
- UK: 2 large potatoes (grated), 2 carrots (grated), 1 zucchini (grated), 1 onion (finely chopped), 2 eggs, 60g all-purpose flour, 5ml baking powder, 5g paprika, salt, pepper, 120ml Greek yogurt, 15ml lemon juice, fresh dill (chopped, for garnish)

Instructions:
1. In a large bowl, combine grated potatoes, carrots, zucchini, and chopped onion.
2. Add eggs, all-purpose flour, baking powder, paprika, salt, and pepper to the bowl, mix well to combine.
3. Preheat your air fryer to 180°C (360°F).
4. Scoop spoonfuls of the vegetable mixture into the air fryer basket, flattening slightly to form fritters.
5. Air fry for 12-15 minutes until golden and crispy, flipping halfway through.
6. In a small bowl, mix together Greek yogurt and lemon juice to make the yogurt sauce.
7. Serve the vegetable fritters hot, garnished with chopped fresh dill and accompanied by yogurt sauce for dipping!

Nutritional Info (per serving): Calories: 200 | Fat: 5g | Carbs: 30g | Protein: 8g

Lentil and Vegetable Shepherd's Pie

Prep: 30 mins | Cook: 40 mins | Serves: 4

Ingredients:
- ❖ US: 200g green lentils, 2 carrots (diced), 2 celery stalks (diced), 1 onion (chopped), 2 cloves garlic (minced), 400g canned tomatoes, 250ml vegetable broth, 500g potatoes (peeled and diced), 60ml milk, 30g butter, salt, pepper, fresh thyme (for garnish)
- ❖ UK: 200g green lentils, 2 carrots (diced), 2 celery stalks (diced), 1 onion (chopped), 2 cloves garlic (minced), 400g canned tomatoes, 250ml vegetable broth, 500g potatoes (peeled and diced), 60ml milk, 30g butter, salt, pepper, fresh thyme (for garnish)

Instructions:
1. Rinse green lentils and cook according to package instructions until tender.
2. In a large skillet, sauté diced carrots, celery, onion, and minced garlic until softened.
3. Add cooked lentils, canned tomatoes, and vegetable broth to the skillet, simmer for 10 minutes.
4. Preheat your air fryer to 180°C (360°F).
5. Meanwhile, boil diced potatoes until fork-tender, then drain.
6. Mash potatoes with milk, butter, salt, and pepper to make mashed potatoes.
7. Transfer the lentil and vegetable mixture to a baking dish.
8. Spread mashed potatoes evenly over the top.
9. Place the baking dish in the air fryer basket.
10. Air fry for 20-25 minutes until the shepherd's pie is heated through and the mashed potatoes are golden brown.
11. Garnish with fresh thyme before serving for a comforting and satisfying meal!

Nutritional Info (per serving): Calories: 350 | Fat: 8g | Carbs: 55g | Protein: 15g

Air-Fried Veggie Burgers

Prep: 20 mins | Cook: 15 mins | Serves: 4

Ingredients:
- ❖ US: 400g mixed beans (kidney beans, black beans), 100g cooked quinoa, 1 onion (chopped), 2 cloves garlic (minced), 30g breadcrumbs, 1 egg, 5ml Worcestershire sauce, 5ml soy sauce, salt, pepper, burger buns, lettuce, tomato, onion slices (for serving)
- ❖ UK: 400g mixed beans (kidney beans, black beans), 100g cooked quinoa, 1 onion (chopped), 2 cloves garlic (minced), 30g breadcrumbs, 1 egg, 5ml Worcestershire sauce, 5ml soy sauce, salt, pepper, burger buns, lettuce, tomato, onion slices (for serving)

Instructions:
1. In a food processor, pulse mixed beans until roughly chopped.
2. In a large bowl, combine chopped beans, cooked quinoa, chopped onion, minced garlic, breadcrumbs, egg, Worcestershire sauce, soy sauce, salt, and pepper.
3. Shape the mixture into burger patties.
4. Preheat your air fryer to 180°C (360°F).
5. Place the burger patties in the air fryer basket.
6. Air fry for 12-15 minutes until golden and crispy, flipping halfway through.
7. Serve the veggie burgers on burger buns with lettuce, tomato, and onion slices for a delicious and satisfying meal!

Nutritional Info (per serving): Calories: 300 | Fat: 5g | Carbs: 45g | Protein: 15g

Stuffed Portobello Mushrooms with Quinoa

Prep: 20 mins | Cook: 20 mins | Serves: 4

Ingredients:
- US: 4 large portobello mushrooms, 100g quinoa (cooked), 1 red bell pepper (diced), 1 yellow bell pepper (diced), 1 onion (diced), 2 cloves garlic (minced), 60g feta cheese (crumbled), 30ml balsamic vinegar, 30ml olive oil, salt, pepper, fresh parsley (for garnish)
- UK: 4 large portobello mushrooms, 100g quinoa (cooked), 1 red bell pepper (diced), 1 yellow bell pepper (diced), 1 onion (diced), 2 cloves garlic (minced), 60g feta cheese (crumbled), 30ml balsamic vinegar, 30ml olive oil, salt, pepper, fresh parsley (for garnish)

Instructions:
1. Remove the stems from the portobello mushrooms and gently scrape out the gills.
2. In a skillet, heat olive oil over medium heat.
3. Sauté diced bell peppers, onion, and minced garlic until softened.
4. Add cooked quinoa to the skillet, stir to combine.
5. Preheat your air fryer to 180°C (360°F).
6. Stuff each portobello mushroom with the quinoa mixture.
7. Drizzle balsamic vinegar over the stuffed mushrooms.
8. Place the stuffed mushrooms in the air fryer basket.
9. Air fry for 15-20 minutes until the mushrooms are tender and the filling is heated through.
10. Sprinkle crumbled feta cheese and fresh parsley over the mushrooms before serving for a delicious and nutritious meal!

Nutritional Info (per serving): Calories: 250 | Fat: 10g | Carbs: 30g | Protein: 10g

Vegetarian Meatless Meatballs in Marinara Sauce

Prep: 30 mins | Cook: 20 mins | Serves: 4

Ingredients:
- US: 200g lentils (cooked), 100g breadcrumbs, 1 onion (finely chopped), 2 cloves garlic (minced), 1 egg, 30g grated Parmesan cheese, 15g fresh parsley (chopped), salt, pepper, 500ml marinara sauce, fresh basil (for garnish)
- UK: 200g lentils (cooked), 100g breadcrumbs, 1 onion (finely chopped), 2 cloves garlic (minced), 1 egg, 30g grated Parmesan cheese, 15g fresh parsley (chopped), salt, pepper, 500ml marinara sauce, fresh basil (for garnish)

Instructions:
1. In a large bowl, combine cooked lentils, breadcrumbs, chopped onion, minced garlic, egg, grated Parmesan cheese, chopped parsley, salt, and pepper.
2. Shape the mixture into meatless meatballs.
3. Preheat your air fryer to 180°C (360°F).
4. Place the meatless meatballs in the air fryer basket.
5. Air fry for 15-20 minutes until golden brown and cooked through, shaking the basket halfway through.
6. In a saucepan, heat marinara sauce over medium heat until warmed.
7. Serve the vegetarian meatless meatballs hot with marinara sauce, garnished with fresh basil for a comforting and flavorful meal!

Nutritional Info (per serving): Calories: 280 | Fat: 8g | Carbs: 35g | Protein: 15g

Air-Fried Tofu Nuggets with Dipping Sauces

Prep: 20 mins | Cook: 15 mins | Serves: 4

Ingredients:
- US: 400g firm tofu, 60g cornstarch, 2 eggs (beaten), 100g breadcrumbs, salt, pepper, cooking spray, dipping sauces of choice (e.g., barbecue sauce, sweet chili sauce, honey mustard)
- UK: 400g firm tofu, 60g cornstarch, 2 eggs (beaten), 100g breadcrumbs, salt, pepper, cooking spray, dipping sauces of choice (e.g., barbecue sauce, sweet chili sauce, honey mustard)

Instructions:
1. Press the tofu to remove excess moisture, then cut into bite-sized nuggets.
2. Set up a breading station with cornstarch, beaten eggs, and breadcrumbs seasoned with salt and pepper.
3. Dip each tofu nugget into the cornstarch, then the beaten eggs, and finally coat with breadcrumbs.
4. Preheat your air fryer to 200°C (400°F).
5. Place the breaded tofu nuggets in the air fryer basket, making sure they are in a single layer.
6. Lightly spray the nuggets with cooking spray.
7. Air fry for 12-15 minutes until golden and crispy, shaking the basket halfway through.
8. Serve the air-fried tofu nuggets hot with a variety of dipping sauces for a fun and delicious meal!

Nutritional Info (per serving): Calories: 250 | Fat: 10g | Carbs: 30g | Protein: 15g

Vegetable Pot Pie with Biscuit Topping

Prep: 30 mins | Cook: 40 mins | Serves: 4

Ingredients:
- US: 2 tablespoons butter, 1 onion (chopped), 2 carrots (diced), 2 celery stalks (diced), 2 cloves garlic (minced), 250g mushrooms (sliced), 60g all-purpose flour, 500ml vegetable broth, 200g frozen peas, 200g frozen corn, 30ml heavy cream, salt, pepper, 1 can refrigerated biscuit dough
- UK: 2 tablespoons butter, 1 onion (chopped), 2 carrots (diced), 2 celery stalks (diced), 2 cloves garlic (minced), 250g mushrooms (sliced), 60g all-purpose flour, 500ml vegetable broth, 200g frozen peas, 200g frozen corn, 30ml heavy cream, salt, pepper, 1 can refrigerated biscuit dough

Instructions:
1. In a large skillet, melt butter over medium heat.
2. Add chopped onion, diced carrots, diced celery, minced garlic, and sliced mushrooms, sauté until softened.
3. Stir in all-purpose flour to coat the vegetables.
4. Gradually pour in vegetable broth, stirring constantly until the mixture thickens.
5. Add frozen peas, frozen corn, and heavy cream to the skillet, stir to combine.
6. Season with salt and pepper to taste.
7. Preheat your air fryer to 180°C (360°F).
8. Transfer the vegetable mixture to a baking dish.
9. Arrange biscuit dough over the top of the vegetable mixture.
10. Place the baking dish in the air fryer basket.
11. Air fry for 25-30 minutes until the biscuit topping is golden brown and the filling is bubbly.
12. Serve the vegetable pot pie hot for a comforting and hearty meal!

Nutritional Info (per serving): Calories: 400 | Fat: 15g | Carbs: 55g | Protein: 10g

Vegan Lentil Loaf with Cranberry Glaze

Prep: 30 mins | Cook: 45 mins | Serves: 4

Ingredients:
- US: 200g green lentils (cooked), 1 onion (chopped), 2 cloves garlic (minced), 1 carrot (grated), 1 celery stalk (finely chopped), 60g breadcrumbs, 30g ground flaxseed, 30ml soy sauce, 15ml tomato paste, salt, pepper, 60ml cranberry sauce
- UK: 200g green lentils (cooked), 1 onion (chopped), 2 cloves garlic (minced), 1 carrot (grated), 1 celery stalk (finely chopped), 60g breadcrumbs, 30g ground flaxseed, 30ml soy sauce, 15ml tomato paste, salt, pepper, 60ml cranberry sauce

Instructions:
1. In a large bowl, mix together cooked green lentils, chopped onion, minced garlic, grated carrot, finely chopped celery, breadcrumbs, ground flaxseed, soy sauce, tomato paste, salt, and pepper.
2. Preheat your air fryer to 180°C (360°F).
3. Press the lentil mixture into a greased loaf pan.
4. Place the loaf pan in the air fryer basket.
5. Air fry for 40-45 minutes until the lentil loaf is firm and golden brown.
6. In a small saucepan, heat cranberry sauce over low heat until warmed.
7. Serve slices of vegan lentil loaf hot with cranberry glaze for a festive and flavorful dish!

Nutritional Info (per serving): Calories: 300 | Fat: 8g | Carbs: 45g | Protein: 12g

Roasted Vegetable Lasagna

Prep: 40 mins | Cook: 45 mins | Serves: 6

Ingredients:
- US: 250g lasagna noodles, 2 zucchinis (sliced), 1 eggplant (sliced), 2 bell peppers (sliced), 1 onion (sliced), 4 cloves garlic (minced), 500ml marinara sauce, 250g ricotta cheese, 250g mozzarella cheese (shredded), 30g grated Parmesan cheese, fresh basil (for garnish), olive oil, salt, pepper
- UK: 250g lasagna noodles, 2 zucchinis (sliced), 1 eggplant (sliced), 2 bell peppers (sliced), 1 onion (sliced), 4 cloves garlic (minced), 500ml marinara sauce, 250g ricotta cheese, 250g mozzarella cheese (shredded), 30g grated Parmesan cheese, fresh basil (for garnish), olive oil, salt, pepper

Instructions:
1. Preheat your oven to 200°C (400°F).
2. Arrange sliced zucchinis, eggplant, bell peppers, onion, and minced garlic on a baking sheet.
3. Drizzle with olive oil and season with salt and pepper.
4. Roast the vegetables in the oven for 20-25 minutes until tender and lightly browned.
5. Cook lasagna noodles according to package instructions until al dente, then drain.
6. In a greased baking dish, spread a layer of marinara sauce on the bottom.
7. Arrange a layer of lasagna noodles over the sauce.
8. Spread ricotta cheese over the noodles, followed by a layer of roasted vegetables.
9. Sprinkle shredded mozzarella cheese and grated Parmesan cheese over the vegetables.
10. Repeat the layers until all ingredients are used, ending with a layer of cheese on top.
11. Cover the baking dish with foil and bake in the oven for 25-30 minutes.
12. Remove the foil and bake for an additional 10-15 minutes until the cheese is bubbly and golden.
13. Let the roasted vegetable lasagna cool slightly before serving, garnished with fresh basil for a delicious and comforting meal!

Nutritional Info (per serving): Calories: 450 | Fat: 20g | Carbs: 45g | Protein: 20g

CHAPTER 7: PASTA AND GRAIN DISHES

Air-Fried Gnocchi with Pesto
Prep: 10 mins | Cook: 15 mins | Serves: 4
Ingredients:
- US: 500g store-bought gnocchi, 60ml pesto sauce, 15ml olive oil, salt, pepper, grated Parmesan cheese (for garnish), fresh basil leaves (for garnish)
- UK: 500g store-bought gnocchi, 60ml pesto sauce, 15ml olive oil, salt, pepper, grated Parmesan cheese (for garnish), fresh basil leaves (for garnish)

Instructions:
1. Preheat your air fryer to 200°C (400°F).
2. Toss gnocchi with olive oil, salt, and pepper in a bowl until coated.
3. Spread gnocchi in a single layer in the air fryer basket.
4. Air fry for 10-12 minutes until golden and crispy, shaking the basket halfway through.
5. Transfer air-fried gnocchi to a serving dish.
6. Drizzle with pesto sauce and toss to coat.
7. Garnish with grated Parmesan cheese and fresh basil leaves before serving.

Nutritional Info (per serving): Calories: 350 | Fat: 15g | Carbs: 45g | Protein: 8g

Vegetable Pasta Bake
Prep: 20 mins | Cook: 40 mins | Serves: 6
Ingredients:
- US: 300g pasta (penne or rigatoni), 1 tablespoon olive oil, 1 onion (chopped), 2 cloves garlic (minced), 2 bell peppers (sliced), 1 zucchini (sliced), 1 eggplant (cubed), 400g canned diced tomatoes, 120ml tomato sauce, 1 teaspoon dried oregano, 1 teaspoon dried basil, salt, pepper, 200g mozzarella cheese (grated), fresh basil leaves (for garnish)
- UK: 300g pasta (penne or rigatoni), 1 tablespoon olive oil, 1 onion (chopped), 2 cloves garlic (minced), 2 bell peppers (sliced), 1 zucchini (sliced), 1 eggplant (cubed), 400g canned diced tomatoes, 120ml tomato sauce, 1 teaspoon dried oregano, 1 teaspoon dried basil, salt, pepper, 200g mozzarella cheese (grated), fresh basil leaves (for garnish)

Instructions:
1. Preheat your oven to 180°C (350°F).
2. Cook pasta according to package instructions until al dente. Drain and set aside.
3. In a large skillet, heat olive oil over medium heat.
4. Add chopped onion and minced garlic, and sauté until softened.
5. Add sliced bell peppers, sliced zucchini, and cubed eggplant to the skillet, and cook until tender.
6. Stir in canned diced tomatoes, tomato sauce, dried oregano, dried basil, salt, and pepper.
7. Add cooked pasta to the skillet and toss to coat with the vegetable mixture.
8. Transfer pasta mixture to a baking dish and sprinkle grated mozzarella cheese on top.
9. Bake for 20-25 minutes until cheese is melted and bubbly.
10. Garnish with fresh basil leaves before serving.

Nutritional Info (per serving): Calories: 400 | Fat: 10g | Carbs: 60g | Protein: 15g

Quinoa Bowls with Roasted Veggies

Prep: 15 mins | Cook: 25 mins | Serves: 4

Ingredients:
- US: 1 cup quinoa, 2 cups water, 1 tablespoon olive oil, 1 red bell pepper (sliced), 1 yellow bell pepper (sliced), 1 zucchini (sliced), 1 red onion (sliced), 1 teaspoon dried thyme, salt, pepper, 100g cherry tomatoes (halved), 60g feta cheese (crumbled), fresh parsley (for garnish)
- UK: 1 cup quinoa, 2 cups water, 1 tablespoon olive oil, 1 red bell pepper (sliced), 1 yellow bell pepper (sliced), 1 zucchini (sliced), 1 red onion (sliced), 1 teaspoon dried thyme, salt, pepper, 100g cherry tomatoes (halved), 60g feta cheese (crumbled), fresh parsley (for garnish)

Instructions:
1. Rinse quinoa under cold water.
2. In a saucepan, bring water to a boil and add quinoa.
3. Reduce heat, cover, and simmer for 15 minutes until quinoa is cooked and water is absorbed. Fluff with a fork and set aside.
4. Preheat your oven to 200°C (400°F).
5. In a large bowl, toss sliced bell peppers, sliced zucchini, sliced red onion, dried thyme, salt, and pepper with olive oil until coated.
6. Spread vegetables on a baking sheet in a single layer.
7. Roast for 20-25 minutes until vegetables are tender and slightly caramelized.
8. Divide cooked quinoa among bowls and top with roasted veggies, cherry tomatoes, and crumbled feta cheese.
9. Garnish with fresh parsley before serving.

Nutritional Info (per serving): Calories: 300 | Fat: 10g | Carbs: 40g | Protein: 10g

Air-Fried Vegetable Fritters over Pasta

Prep: 20 mins | Cook: 20 mins | Serves: 4

Ingredients:
- US: 2 cups shredded mixed vegetables (carrots, zucchini, bell peppers), 2 eggs, 60g breadcrumbs, 30g grated Parmesan cheese, 2 tablespoons chopped fresh parsley, salt, pepper, 200g pasta, 120ml marinara sauce, fresh basil leaves (for garnish)
- UK: 2 cups shredded mixed vegetables (carrots, zucchini, bell peppers), 2 eggs, 60g breadcrumbs, 30g grated Parmesan cheese, 2 tablespoons chopped fresh parsley, salt, pepper, 200g pasta, 120ml marinara sauce, fresh basil leaves (for garnish)

Instructions:
1. In a large bowl, combine shredded mixed vegetables, eggs, breadcrumbs, grated Parmesan cheese, chopped fresh parsley, salt, and pepper.
2. Heat olive oil in a skillet over medium heat.
3. Scoop vegetable mixture and form into patties.
4. Fry vegetable fritters in the skillet until golden brown and cooked through, about 3-4 minutes per side.
5. Cook pasta according to package instructions until al dente. Drain and set aside.
6. In a separate saucepan, heat marinara sauce until warmed through.
7. Preheat your air fryer to 200°C (400°F).
8. Place cooked vegetable fritters in the air fryer basket and air fry for 5-7 minutes until crispy.
9. Serve vegetable fritters over cooked pasta, drizzle with marinara sauce, and garnish with fresh basil leaves.

Nutritional Info (per serving): Calories: 350 | Fat: 10g | Carbs: 50g | Protein: 15g

Vegan Mac and Cheese

Prep: 15 mins | Cook: 20 mins | Serves: 4

Ingredients:
- US: 300g macaroni pasta, 2 cups peeled and cubed potatoes, 1 cup peeled and chopped carrots, 1/2 cup nutritional yeast, 1/4 cup olive oil, 1/4 cup unsweetened almond milk, 1 tablespoon lemon juice, 1 teaspoon garlic powder, 1 teaspoon onion powder, salt, pepper, fresh parsley (for garnish)
- UK: 300g macaroni pasta, 2 cups peeled and cubed potatoes, 1 cup peeled and chopped carrots, 1/2 cup nutritional yeast, 1/4 cup olive oil, 1/4 cup unsweetened almond milk, 1 tablespoon lemon juice, 1 teaspoon garlic powder, 1 teaspoon onion powder, salt, pepper, fresh parsley (for garnish)

Instructions:
1. Cook macaroni pasta according to package instructions until al dente. Drain and set aside.
2. In a pot, bring water to a boil and add cubed potatoes and chopped carrots.
3. Boil until vegetables are tender, about 10-15 minutes. Drain and set aside.
4. In a blender, combine cooked potatoes, cooked carrots, nutritional yeast, olive oil, almond milk, lemon juice, garlic powder, onion powder, salt, and pepper. Blend until smooth and creamy.
5. Toss cooked macaroni pasta with the vegan cheese sauce until evenly coated.
6. Heat the mac and cheese on the stovetop until warmed through.
7. Serve vegan mac and cheese hot, garnished with fresh parsley.

Nutritional Info (per serving): Calories: 350 | Fat: 15g | Carbs: 50g | Protein: 10g

Lentil Bolognese over Zucchini Noodles

Prep: 15 mins | Cook: 30 mins | Serves: 4

Ingredients:
- US: 2 tablespoons olive oil, 1 onion (chopped), 2 cloves garlic (minced), 200g cooked lentils, 400g canned diced tomatoes, 120ml tomato sauce, 1 teaspoon dried oregano, 1 teaspoon dried basil, salt, pepper, 4 medium zucchinis (spiralized), fresh parsley (for garnish)
- UK: 2 tablespoons olive oil, 1 onion (chopped), 2 cloves garlic (minced), 200g cooked lentils, 400g canned diced tomatoes, 120ml tomato sauce, 1 teaspoon dried oregano, 1 teaspoon dried basil, salt, pepper, 4 medium zucchinis (spiralized), fresh parsley (for garnish)

Instructions:
1. In a large skillet, heat olive oil over medium heat.
2. Add chopped onion and minced garlic, and sauté until softened.
3. Stir in cooked lentils, canned diced tomatoes, tomato sauce, dried oregano, dried basil, salt, and pepper.
4. Simmer for 20-25 minutes until sauce is thickened.
5. Meanwhile, spiralize zucchinis into noodles.
6. Heat a separate skillet over medium heat and add zucchini noodles.
7. Sauté for 3-4 minutes until noodles are tender.
8. Serve lentil bolognese over zucchini noodles, garnished with fresh parsley.

Nutritional Info (per serving): Calories: 250 | Fat: 10g | Carbs: 30g | Protein: 10g

Mediterranean Couscous Salad

Prep: 15 mins | Cook: 10 mins | Serves: 4

Ingredients:
- US: 1 cup couscous, 1 1/4 cups vegetable broth, 1 tablespoon olive oil, 1 lemon (juiced), 1 teaspoon Dijon mustard, 1 clove garlic (minced), salt, pepper, 1 cucumber (diced), 1 bell pepper (diced), 100g cherry tomatoes (halved), 60g Kalamata olives (pitted and sliced), 60g feta cheese (crumbled), fresh parsley (for garnish)
- UK: 1 cup couscous, 1 1/4 cups vegetable broth, 1 tablespoon olive oil, 1 lemon (juiced), 1 teaspoon Dijon mustard, 1 clove garlic (minced), salt, pepper, 1 cucumber (diced), 1 bell pepper (diced), 100g cherry tomatoes (halved), 60g Kalamata olives (pitted and sliced), 60g feta cheese (crumbled), fresh parsley (for garnish)

Instructions:
1. In a saucepan, bring vegetable broth to a boil.
2. Stir in couscous, cover, and remove from heat. Let stand for 5 minutes.
3. Fluff couscous with a fork and transfer to a large bowl.
4. In a small bowl, whisk together olive oil, lemon juice, Dijon mustard, minced garlic, salt, and pepper to make the dressing.
5. Pour dressing over couscous and toss to coat.
6. Add diced cucumber, diced bell pepper, halved cherry tomatoes, sliced Kalamata olives, and crumbled feta cheese to the couscous mixture.
7. Toss until evenly combined.
8. Garnish with fresh parsley before serving.

Nutritional Info (per serving): Calories: 300 | Fat: 10g | Carbs: 45g | Protein: 10g

Stuffed Pasta Shells with Spinach and Ricotta

Prep: 20 mins | Cook: 25 mins | Serves: 4

Ingredients:
- US: 200g jumbo pasta shells, 200g ricotta cheese, 100g frozen chopped spinach (thawed and drained), 1 egg, 30g grated Parmesan cheese, 1/2 teaspoon garlic powder, salt, pepper, 480ml marinara sauce, fresh basil leaves (for garnish)
- UK: 200g jumbo pasta shells, 200g ricotta cheese, 100g frozen chopped spinach (thawed and drained), 1 egg, 30g grated Parmesan cheese, 1/2 teaspoon garlic powder, salt, pepper, 480ml marinara sauce, fresh basil leaves (for garnish)

Instructions:
1. Cook jumbo pasta shells according to package instructions until al dente. Drain and set aside.
2. In a bowl, combine ricotta cheese, thawed and drained chopped spinach, egg, grated Parmesan cheese, garlic powder, salt, and pepper.
3. Preheat your oven to 180°C (350°F).
4. Stuff cooked pasta shells with the spinach and ricotta mixture.
5. Spread marinara sauce in the bottom of a baking dish.
6. Arrange stuffed pasta shells in the baking dish.
7. Cover with foil and bake for 20 minutes.
8. Remove foil and bake for an additional 5 minutes until heated through.
9. Garnish with fresh basil leaves before serving.

Nutritional Info (per serving): Calories: 350 | Fat: 10g | Carbs: 45g | Protein: 15g

Air-Fried Veggie Meatballs with Spaghetti

Prep: 15 mins | Cook: 20 mins | Serves: 4

Ingredients:
- US: 1 cup cooked quinoa, 200g cooked lentils, 1 carrot (grated), 1 zucchini (grated), 1 onion (finely chopped), 2 cloves garlic (minced), 30g breadcrumbs, 1 tablespoon tomato paste, 1 teaspoon dried oregano, 1 teaspoon dried basil, salt, pepper, olive oil spray, 200g spaghetti, 480ml marinara sauce, fresh basil leaves (for garnish)
- UK: 1 cup cooked quinoa, 200g cooked lentils, 1 carrot (grated), 1 zucchini (grated), 1 onion (finely chopped), 2 cloves garlic (minced), 30g breadcrumbs, 1 tablespoon tomato paste, 1 teaspoon dried oregano, 1 teaspoon dried basil, salt, pepper, olive oil spray, 200g spaghetti, 480ml marinara sauce, fresh basil leaves (for garnish)

Instructions:
1. Preheat your air fryer to 180°C (350°F).
2. In a large bowl, combine cooked quinoa, cooked lentils, grated carrot, grated zucchini, chopped onion, minced garlic, breadcrumbs, tomato paste, dried oregano, dried basil, salt, and pepper.
3. Use your hands to mix until well combined.
4. Shape mixture into small meatballs.
5. Lightly spray meatballs with olive oil spray.
6. Place meatballs in the air fryer basket in a single layer.
7. Air fry for 15-20 minutes until golden brown and cooked through.
8. Meanwhile, cook spaghetti according to package instructions until al dente. Drain and set aside.
9. Heat marinara sauce in a saucepan until warmed through.
10. Serve veggie meatballs over cooked spaghetti, topped with marinara sauce and fresh basil leaves.

Nutritional Info (per serving): Calories: 400 | Fat: 10g | Carbs: 60g | Protein: 15g

Mushroom Risotto with Crispy Air-Fried Leeks

Prep: 15 mins | Cook: 30 mins | Serves: 4

Ingredients:
- US: 1 tablespoon olive oil, 1 onion (chopped), 2 cloves garlic (minced), 200g Arborio rice, 120ml white wine, 4 cups vegetable broth, 200g mushrooms (sliced), 30g grated Parmesan cheese, salt, pepper, 2 leeks (sliced into thin rounds), olive oil spray
- UK: 1 tablespoon olive oil, 1 onion (chopped), 2 cloves garlic (minced), 200g Arborio rice, 120ml white wine, 4 cups vegetable broth, 200g mushrooms (sliced), 30g grated Parmesan cheese, salt, pepper, 2 leeks (sliced into thin rounds), olive oil spray

Instructions:
1. In a large skillet, heat olive oil over medium heat.
2. Add chopped onion and minced garlic, and sauté until softened.
3. Stir in Arborio rice and cook for 1-2 minutes until translucent.
4. Deglaze the skillet with white wine and cook until absorbed.
5. Gradually add vegetable broth, 1 cup at a time, stirring frequently and allowing each addition to be absorbed before adding more.
6. In a separate skillet, sauté sliced mushrooms until tender.
7. Once the risotto is creamy and rice is cooked through, stir in sautéed mushrooms and grated Parmesan cheese.
8. Season with salt and pepper to taste.

9. Preheat your air fryer to 200°C (400°F).
10. Spread sliced leeks in a single layer in the air fryer basket and spray with olive oil.
11. Air fry for 5-7 minutes until crispy.
12. Serve mushroom risotto topped with crispy air-fried leeks.

Nutritional Info (per serving): Calories: 350 | Fat: 10g | Carbs: 55g | Protein: 10g

CHAPTER 8: PIZZA AND FLATBREADS

Air-Fried Veggie Pizza
Prep: 15 mins | Cook: 12 mins | Serves: 2
Ingredients:
- US: 2 naan breads, 120ml marinara sauce, 100g mozzarella cheese (shredded), 1 bell pepper (sliced), 1/2 red onion (sliced), 1 tomato (sliced), 60g black olives (sliced), 30g feta cheese (crumbled), fresh basil leaves (for garnish)
- UK: 2 naan breads, 120ml marinara sauce, 100g mozzarella cheese (shredded), 1 bell pepper (sliced), 1/2 red onion (sliced), 1 tomato (sliced), 60g black olives (sliced), 30g feta cheese (crumbled), fresh basil leaves (for garnish)

Instructions:
1. Preheat your air fryer to 200°C (400°F).
2. Spread marinara sauce evenly over each naan bread.
3. Sprinkle shredded mozzarella cheese over the sauce.
4. Arrange sliced bell pepper, red onion, tomato, and black olives on top of the cheese.
5. Crumble feta cheese over the veggies.
6. Place the prepared pizzas in the air fryer basket.
7. Air fry for 10-12 minutes until the crust is crisp and the cheese is melted and bubbly.
8. Garnish with fresh basil leaves before serving for a delicious and satisfying pizza experience!

Nutritional Info (per serving): Calories: 450 | Fat: 20g | Carbs: 50g | Protein: 15g

Naan Bread Pizzas with Roasted Veggies
Prep: 15 mins | Cook: 15 mins | Serves: 2
Ingredients:
- US: 2 naan breads, 120ml marinara sauce, 100g mozzarella cheese (shredded), 1 zucchini (sliced), 1 bell pepper (sliced), 1 red onion (sliced), 60g cherry tomatoes (halved), 30ml olive oil, salt, pepper, fresh basil leaves (for garnish)
- UK: 2 naan breads, 120ml marinara sauce, 100g mozzarella cheese (shredded), 1 zucchini (sliced), 1 bell pepper (sliced), 1 red onion (sliced), 60g cherry tomatoes (halved), 30ml olive oil, salt, pepper, fresh basil leaves (for garnish)

Instructions:
1. Preheat your air fryer to 200°C (400°F).
2. Toss sliced zucchini, bell pepper, red onion, and cherry tomatoes with olive oil, salt, and pepper.
3. Spread marinara sauce evenly over each naan bread.
4. Sprinkle shredded mozzarella cheese over the sauce.
5. Arrange the roasted veggies on top of the cheese.
6. Place the prepared pizzas in the air fryer basket.
7. Air fry for 10-12 minutes until the crust is golden and crisp and the cheese is melted.
8. Garnish with fresh basil leaves before serving for a delicious and nutritious pizza treat!

Nutritional Info (per serving): Calories: 400 | Fat: 15g | Carbs: 55g | Protein: 15g

Flatbread Wraps with Falafel and Veggies

Prep: 20 mins | Cook: 15 mins | Serves: 4

Ingredients:
- US: 4 flatbreads, 200g falafel, 100g hummus, 1 cucumber (sliced), 1 tomato (sliced), 1/2 red onion (sliced), 60g mixed salad greens, 30ml tahini sauce, fresh parsley (for garnish)
- UK: 4 flatbreads, 200g falafel, 100g hummus, 1 cucumber (sliced), 1 tomato (sliced), 1/2 red onion (sliced), 60g mixed salad greens, 30ml tahini sauce, fresh parsley (for garnish)

Instructions:
1. Preheat your air fryer to 180°C (360°F).
2. Heat the falafel according to package instructions until warm and crisp.
3. Warm the flatbreads in the air fryer for a few minutes.
4. Spread hummus evenly over each flatbread.
5. Place falafel, sliced cucumber, tomato, red onion, and mixed salad greens on one side of each flatbread.
6. Drizzle tahini sauce over the fillings.
7. Fold the flatbreads over the fillings to form wraps.
8. Garnish with fresh parsley before serving for a flavorful and satisfying meal!

Nutritional Info (per serving): Calories: 350 | Fat: 15g | Carbs: 45g | Protein: 15g

Air-Fried Calzones with Spinach and Feta

Prep: 30 mins | Cook: 15 mins | Serves: 4

Ingredients:
- US: 500g pizza dough, 200g frozen spinach (thawed and drained), 100g feta cheese (crumbled), 100g mozzarella cheese (shredded), 60ml marinara sauce, 1 egg (beaten), olive oil (for brushing), salt, pepper, dried oregano (for garnish)
- UK: 500g pizza dough, 200g frozen spinach (thawed and drained), 100g feta cheese (crumbled), 100g mozzarella cheese (shredded), 60ml marinara sauce, 1 egg (beaten), olive oil (for brushing), salt, pepper, dried oregano (for garnish)

Instructions:
1. Preheat your air fryer to 200°C (400°F).
2. Divide pizza dough into 4 equal portions.
3. Roll out each portion into a circle on a floured surface.
4. In a bowl, mix together thawed and drained spinach, crumbled feta cheese, shredded mozzarella cheese, marinara sauce, salt, and pepper.
5. Place a portion of the spinach and cheese mixture on one half of each dough circle.
6. Fold the other half of the dough over the filling to form calzones.
7. Press the edges firmly to seal.
8. Brush the tops of the calzones with beaten egg and sprinkle with dried oregano.
9. Place the calzones in the air fryer basket.
10. Air fry for 12-15 minutes until golden brown and crispy.
11. Serve the air-fried calzones hot for a delicious and comforting meal!

Nutritional Info (per serving): Calories: 400 | Fat: 15g | Carbs: 55g | Protein: 15g

Grilled Vegetable and Pesto Pizza

Prep: 20 mins | Cook: 15 mins | Serves: 2

Ingredients:
- US: 2 pre-made pizza crusts, 120ml pesto sauce, 100g mozzarella cheese (shredded), 1 zucchini (sliced), 1 yellow squash (sliced), 1 red onion (sliced), 60g cherry tomatoes (halved), 30ml olive oil, salt, pepper, fresh basil leaves (for garnish)
- UK: 2 pre-made pizza crusts, 120ml pesto sauce, 100g mozzarella cheese (shredded), 1 zucchini (sliced), 1 yellow squash (sliced), 1 red onion (sliced), 60g cherry tomatoes (halved), 30ml olive oil, salt, pepper, fresh basil leaves (for garnish)

Instructions:
1. Preheat your air fryer to 200°C (400°F).
2. Toss sliced zucchini, yellow squash, red onion, and cherry tomatoes with olive oil, salt, and pepper.
3. Grill the vegetables in the air fryer for 8-10 minutes until tender and lightly charred.
4. Spread pesto sauce evenly over each pizza crust.
5. Sprinkle shredded mozzarella cheese over the sauce.
6. Arrange the grilled vegetables on top of the cheese.
7. Place the prepared pizzas in the air fryer basket.
8. Air fry for 10-12 minutes until the crust is crisp and the cheese is melted and bubbly.
9. Garnish with fresh basil leaves before serving for a delightful and flavorful pizza experience!

Nutritional Info (per serving): Calories: 450 | Fat: 20g | Carbs: 45g | Protein: 15g

Vegan BBQ Jackfruit Flatbread

Prep: 20 mins | Cook: 20 mins | Serves: 2

Ingredients:
- US: 2 flatbreads, 200g canned jackfruit (drained and shredded), 120ml barbecue sauce, 1/2 red onion (sliced), 1/2 bell pepper (sliced), 60g corn kernels, 30g vegan cheese (shredded), fresh cilantro (for garnish)
- UK: 2 flatbreads, 200g canned jackfruit (drained and shredded), 120ml barbecue sauce, 1/2 red onion (sliced), 1/2 bell pepper (sliced), 60g corn kernels, 30g vegan cheese (shredded), fresh cilantro (for garnish)

Instructions:
1. Preheat your air fryer to 180°C (360°F).
2. In a bowl, mix together shredded jackfruit and barbecue sauce until well coated.
3. Spread the barbecue jackfruit mixture evenly over each flatbread.
4. Top with sliced red onion, bell pepper, and corn kernels.
5. Sprinkle shredded vegan cheese over the toppings.
6. Place the prepared flatbreads in the air fryer basket.
7. Air fry for 15-20 minutes until the crust is golden and crisp.
8. Garnish with fresh cilantro before serving for a tasty and satisfying flatbread!

Nutritional Info (per serving): Calories: 400 | Fat: 15g | Carbs: 55g | Protein: 10g

Air-Fried Garlic Knots

Prep: 15 mins | Cook: 10 mins | Serves: 4

Ingredients:
- US: 500g pizza dough, 30g butter (melted), 2 cloves garlic (minced), 15ml olive oil, 15g grated Parmesan cheese, 5g dried parsley, salt
- UK: 500g pizza dough, 30g butter (melted), 2 cloves garlic (minced), 15ml olive oil, 15g grated Parmesan cheese, 5g dried parsley, salt

Instructions:
1. Preheat your air fryer to 180°C (360°F).
2. Divide pizza dough into 16 equal portions.
3. Roll each portion into a rope and tie into knots.
4. In a bowl, mix together melted butter, minced garlic, olive oil, grated Parmesan cheese, dried parsley, and a pinch of salt.
5. Dip each knot into the garlic butter mixture, coating evenly.
6. Place the garlic knots in the air fryer basket.
7. Air fry for 8-10 minutes until golden brown and cooked through.
8. Serve the air-fried garlic knots hot as a delicious and aromatic appetizer or side dish!

Nutritional Info (per serving): Calories: 250 | Fat: 10g | Carbs: 35g | Protein: 5g

Mediterranean Veggie Stromboli

Prep: 30 mins | Cook: 25 mins | Serves: 4

Ingredients:
- US: 500g pizza dough, 120ml marinara sauce, 100g mozzarella cheese (shredded), 1/2 red bell pepper (sliced), 1/2 yellow bell pepper (sliced), 1/2 red onion (sliced), 60g black olives (sliced), 60g artichoke hearts (chopped), 30ml olive oil, salt, pepper, dried oregano (for garnish)
- UK: 500g pizza dough, 120ml marinara sauce, 100g mozzarella cheese (shredded), 1/2 red bell pepper (sliced), 1/2 yellow bell pepper (sliced), 1/2 red onion (sliced), 60g black olives (sliced), 60g artichoke hearts (chopped), 30ml olive oil, salt, pepper, dried oregano (for garnish)

Instructions:
1. Preheat your air fryer to 200°C (400°F).
2. Roll out pizza dough into a large rectangle on a floured surface.
3. Spread marinara sauce evenly over the dough, leaving a border around the edges.
4. Sprinkle shredded mozzarella cheese over the sauce.
5. Arrange sliced bell peppers, red onion, black olives, and chopped artichoke hearts on top of the cheese.
6. Drizzle olive oil over the vegetables and season with salt, pepper, and dried oregano.
7. Roll up the dough tightly into a log, starting from one long edge.
8. Place the stromboli seam side down in the air fryer basket.
9. Air fry for 20-25 minutes until the crust is golden and crispy.
10. Let the Mediterranean veggie stromboli cool slightly before slicing and serving for a delicious and satisfying meal!

Nutritional Info (per serving): Calories: 400 | Fat: 15g | Carbs: 55g | Protein: 15g

Caprese Flatbread with Balsamic Glaze

Prep: 15 mins | Cook: 15 mins | Serves: 2

Ingredients:
- US: 2 flatbreads, 120ml balsamic glaze, 100g mozzarella cheese (sliced), 2 tomatoes (sliced), 30g fresh basil leaves, 15ml olive oil, salt, pepper
- UK: 2 flatbreads, 120ml balsamic glaze, 100g mozzarella cheese (sliced), 2 tomatoes (sliced), 30g fresh basil leaves, 15ml olive oil, salt, pepper

Instructions:
1. Preheat your air fryer to 200°C (400°F).
2. Place flatbreads in the air fryer basket.
3. Drizzle olive oil over the flatbreads and season with salt and pepper.
4. Air fry for 3-5 minutes until the flatbreads are lightly toasted.
5. Remove the flatbreads from the air fryer and top with sliced mozzarella cheese and tomato.
6. Return the flatbreads to the air fryer and air fry for another 3-5 minutes until the cheese is melted and bubbly.
7. Arrange fresh basil leaves over the melted cheese.
8. Drizzle balsamic glaze over the Caprese flatbreads before serving for a delightful and refreshing appetizer or light meal!

Nutritional Info (per serving): Calories: 350 | Fat: 15g | Carbs: 45g | Protein: 10g

Mexican-Inspired Veggie Pizzas

Prep: 20 mins | Cook: 15 mins | Serves: 2

Ingredients:
- US: 2 pre-made pizza crusts, 120ml salsa, 100g cheddar cheese (shredded), 1/2 red bell pepper (sliced), 1/2 yellow bell pepper (sliced), 1/2 red onion (sliced), 60g black beans (cooked), 30g sliced jalapeños, fresh cilantro (for garnish)
- UK: 2 pre-made pizza crusts, 120ml salsa, 100g cheddar cheese (shredded), 1/2 red bell pepper (sliced), 1/2 yellow bell pepper (sliced), 1/2 red onion (sliced), 60g black beans (cooked), 30g sliced jalapeños, fresh cilantro (for garnish)

Instructions:
1. Preheat your air fryer to 200°C (400°F).
2. Spread salsa evenly over each pizza crust.
3. Sprinkle shredded cheddar cheese over the salsa.
4. Arrange sliced bell peppers, red onion, black beans, and jalapeños on top of the cheese.
5. Place the prepared pizzas in the air fryer basket.
6. Air fry for 10-12 minutes until the crust is crisp and the cheese is melted and bubbly.
7. Garnish with fresh cilantro before serving for a spicy and flavorful pizza experience!

Nutritional Info (per serving): Calories: 400 | Fat: 15g | Carbs: 45g | Protein: 15g

CHAPTER 9: DESSERTS AND BAKED GOODS

Air-Fried Fruit Crisps (Apple, Berry, Peach)
Prep: 10 mins | Cook: 15 mins | Serves: 4
Ingredients:
- US: 2 apples (cored and sliced), 1 cup mixed berries, 2 peaches (sliced), 30g rolled oats, 15g almond flour, 15g coconut oil (melted), 1 tablespoon maple syrup, 1/2 teaspoon ground cinnamon, pinch of salt
- UK: 2 apples (cored and sliced), 1 cup mixed berries, 2 peaches (sliced), 30g rolled oats, 15g almond flour, 15g coconut oil (melted), 1 tablespoon maple syrup, 1/2 teaspoon ground cinnamon, pinch of salt

Instructions:
1. Preheat your air fryer to 180°C (350°F).
2. In a bowl, combine sliced apples, mixed berries, and sliced peaches.
3. In another bowl, mix rolled oats, almond flour, melted coconut oil, maple syrup, ground cinnamon, and a pinch of salt to make the crumble topping.
4. Divide the fruit mixture into individual ramekins.
5. Sprinkle the crumble topping evenly over the fruit.
6. Place the ramekins in the air fryer basket and air fry for 12-15 minutes until the topping is golden and the fruit is bubbling.
7. Serve the fruit crisps hot, optionally with a scoop of ice cream or a dollop of whipped cream.

Nutritional Info (per serving): Calories: 150 | Fat: 5g | Carbs: 25g | Protein: 2g

Baked Apples with Oat Crumble Topping
Prep: 15 mins | Cook: 25 mins | Serves: 4
Ingredients:
- US: 4 apples (cored), 30g rolled oats, 15g almond flour, 15g coconut oil (melted), 1 tablespoon maple syrup, 1/2 teaspoon ground cinnamon, pinch of nutmeg, pinch of salt
- UK: 4 apples (cored), 30g rolled oats, 15g almond flour, 15g coconut oil (melted), 1 tablespoon maple syrup, 1/2 teaspoon ground cinnamon, pinch of nutmeg, pinch of salt

Instructions:
1. Preheat your oven to 180°C (350°F).
2. Place cored apples in a baking dish.
3. In a bowl, mix rolled oats, almond flour, melted coconut oil, maple syrup, ground cinnamon, nutmeg, and a pinch of salt to make the crumble topping.
4. Stuff each cored apple with the crumble topping mixture.
5. Bake for 20-25 minutes until the apples are tender and the topping is golden brown.
6. Serve the baked apples hot, optionally with a drizzle of caramel sauce or a scoop of vanilla ice cream.

Nutritional Info (per serving): Calories: 200 | Fat: 7g | Carbs: 35g | Protein: 2g

Vegan Banana Bread

Prep: 15 mins | Cook: 50 mins | Serves: 8

Ingredients:
- US: 3 ripe bananas, 120ml maple syrup, 60ml coconut oil (melted), 1 teaspoon vanilla extract, 240g all-purpose flour, 1 teaspoon baking powder, 1/2 teaspoon baking soda, 1/2 teaspoon ground cinnamon, pinch of salt, 60ml almond milk, 60g chopped walnuts (optional)
- UK: 3 ripe bananas, 120ml maple syrup, 60ml coconut oil (melted), 1 teaspoon vanilla extract, 240g all-purpose flour, 1 teaspoon baking powder, 1/2 teaspoon baking soda, 1/2 teaspoon ground cinnamon, pinch of salt, 60ml almond milk, 60g chopped walnuts (optional)

Instructions:
1. Preheat your oven to 180°C (350°F). Grease a loaf pan and set aside.
2. In a mixing bowl, mash ripe bananas with a fork until smooth.
3. Add maple syrup, melted coconut oil, and vanilla extract to the mashed bananas, and mix until well combined.
4. In a separate bowl, sift together all-purpose flour, baking powder, baking soda, ground cinnamon, and a pinch of salt.
5. Gradually add the dry ingredients to the wet ingredients, alternating with almond milk, and mix until just combined. Do not overmix.
6. Fold in chopped walnuts if using.
7. Pour the batter into the prepared loaf pan and smooth the top with a spatula.
8. Bake for 45-50 minutes until a toothpick inserted into the center comes out clean.
9. Allow the banana bread to cool in the pan for 10 minutes before transferring it to a wire rack to cool completely.
10. Slice and serve the vegan banana bread as a delicious snack or dessert.

Nutritional Info (per serving): Calories: 250 | Fat: 10g | Carbs: 35g | Protein: 3g

Air-Fried Veggie Muffins (Carrot, Zucchini, Pumpkin)

Prep: 15 mins | Cook: 20 mins | Makes: 12 muffins

Ingredients:
- US: 200g all-purpose flour, 1 teaspoon baking powder, 1/2 teaspoon baking soda, 1/2 teaspoon ground cinnamon, 1/4 teaspoon ground nutmeg, 1/4 teaspoon ground ginger, 1/4 teaspoon salt, 2 eggs, 120ml maple syrup, 60ml coconut oil (melted), 120ml unsweetened applesauce, 1 teaspoon vanilla extract, 100g grated carrot, 100g grated zucchini, 100g canned pumpkin puree
- UK: 200g all-purpose flour, 1 teaspoon baking powder, 1/2 teaspoon baking soda, 1/2 teaspoon ground cinnamon, 1/4 teaspoon ground nutmeg, 1/4 teaspoon ground ginger, 1/4 teaspoon salt, 2 eggs, 120ml maple syrup, 60ml coconut oil (melted), 120ml unsweetened applesauce, 1 teaspoon vanilla extract, 100g grated carrot, 100g grated zucchini, 100g canned pumpkin puree

Instructions:
1. Preheat your air fryer to 180°C (350°F). Line a muffin tin with paper liners and set aside.
2. In a large bowl, whisk together all-purpose flour, baking powder, baking soda, ground cinnamon, ground nutmeg, ground ginger, and salt.
3. In another bowl, beat eggs, maple syrup, melted coconut oil, unsweetened applesauce, and vanilla extract until well combined.
4. Pour the wet ingredients into the dry ingredients and mix until just combined.
5. Fold in grated carrot, grated zucchini, and pumpkin puree until evenly distributed.
6. Spoon the batter into the prepared muffin tin, filling each muffin cup about 2/3 full.

7. Place the muffin tin in the air fryer basket and air fry for 18-20 minutes until a toothpick inserted into the center of a muffin comes out clean.
8. Remove the muffins from the air fryer and allow them to cool in the tin for 5 minutes before transferring them to a wire rack to cool completely.
9. Enjoy these nutritious veggie muffins as a wholesome snack or breakfast treat.

Nutritional Info (per serving):   Calories: 150 | Fat: 5g | Carbs: 25g | Protein: 3g

Chocolate Avocado Mousse

Prep: 10 mins | Chill: 1 hour | Serves: 4

Ingredients:
- US: 2 ripe avocados, 60g unsweetened cocoa powder, 120ml maple syrup, 1 teaspoon vanilla extract, pinch of salt, fresh berries (for garnish)
- UK: 2 ripe avocados, 60g unsweetened cocoa powder, 120ml maple syrup, 1 teaspoon vanilla extract, pinch of salt, fresh berries (for garnish)

Instructions:
1. In a blender or food processor, combine ripe avocados, unsweetened cocoa powder, maple syrup, vanilla extract, and a pinch of salt.
2. Blend until smooth and creamy, scraping down the sides as needed.
3. Divide the chocolate avocado mousse into individual serving cups or glasses.
4. Cover and refrigerate for at least 1 hour to chill and set.
5. Before serving, garnish with fresh berries.
6. Enjoy this indulgent yet healthy chocolate dessert guilt-free.

Nutritional Info (per serving):   Calories: 200 | Fat: 15g | Carbs: 20g | Protein: 3g

Air-Fried Doughnuts with Fruit Glazes

Prep: 15 mins | Cook: 10 mins | Serves: 6

Ingredients:
- US: 200g all-purpose flour, 60g granulated sugar, 1 teaspoon baking powder, 1/4 teaspoon baking soda, 1/4 teaspoon ground nutmeg, pinch of salt, 120ml buttermilk, 1 egg, 30g unsalted butter (melted), 1 teaspoon vanilla extract, olive oil spray
- UK: 200g all-purpose flour, 60g granulated sugar, 1 teaspoon baking powder, 1/4 teaspoon baking soda, 1/4 teaspoon ground nutmeg, pinch of salt, 120ml buttermilk, 1 egg, 30g unsalted butter (melted), 1 teaspoon vanilla extract, olive oil spray

Instructions:
1. Preheat your air fryer to 180°C (350°F). Lightly grease a doughnut pan with olive oil spray and set aside.
2. In a mixing bowl, whisk together all-purpose flour, granulated sugar, baking powder, baking soda, ground nutmeg, and a pinch of salt.
3. In another bowl, whisk together buttermilk, egg, melted unsalted butter, and vanilla extract.
4. Pour the wet ingredients into the dry ingredients and mix until just combined.
5. Spoon the batter into the prepared doughnut pan, filling each cavity about 2/3 full.
6. Place the doughnut pan in the air fryer basket and air fry for 8-10 minutes until the doughnuts are golden brown and cooked through.
7. Remove the doughnuts from the air fryer and allow them to cool in the pan for a few minutes before transferring them to a wire rack to cool completely.
8. Once cooled, glaze the doughnuts with your favorite fruit glazes or toppings.
9. Serve these delightful air-fried doughnuts as a tasty treat for breakfast or dessert.

Nutritional Info (per serving):   Calories: 200 | Fat: 5g | Carbs: 35g | Protein: 4g

Vegan Brownies
Prep: 15 mins | Cook: 25 mins | Serves: 9
Ingredients:
- US: 120g all-purpose flour, 60g unsweetened cocoa powder, 1/2 teaspoon baking powder, 1/4 teaspoon baking soda, pinch of salt, 120ml maple syrup, 60ml coconut oil (melted), 1 teaspoon vanilla extract, 120g unsweetened applesauce, 60g dairy-free chocolate chips
- UK: 120g all-purpose flour, 60g unsweetened cocoa powder, 1/2 teaspoon baking powder, 1/4 teaspoon baking soda, pinch of salt, 120ml maple syrup, 60ml coconut oil (melted), 1 teaspoon vanilla extract, 120g unsweetened applesauce, 60g dairy-free chocolate chips

Instructions:
1. Preheat your oven to 180°C (350°F). Grease an 8x8-inch baking pan and line it with parchment paper, leaving an overhang on the sides for easy removal.
2. In a mixing bowl, whisk together all-purpose flour, unsweetened cocoa powder, baking powder, baking soda, and a pinch of salt.
3. In another bowl, whisk together maple syrup, melted coconut oil, vanilla extract, and unsweetened applesauce until well combined.
4. Pour the wet ingredients into the dry ingredients and mix until just combined.
5. Fold in dairy-free chocolate chips.
6. Transfer the batter to the prepared baking pan and spread it evenly.
7. Bake for 20-25 minutes until the edges are set and a toothpick inserted into the center comes out with a few moist crumbs.
8. Allow the brownies to cool completely in the pan on a wire rack before slicing and serving.
9. Enjoy these decadent vegan brownies as a delightful dessert or snack.

Nutritional Info (per serving):   Calories: 200 | Fat: 10g | Carbs: 25g | Protein: 3g

Air-Fried Cinnamon Sugar Churros
Prep: 15 mins | Cook: 10 mins | Serves: 4
Ingredients:
- US: 120ml water, 60g unsalted butter, 2 tablespoons granulated sugar, 1/4 teaspoon salt, 120g all-purpose flour, 1 egg, 1/2 teaspoon vanilla extract, olive oil spray, 60g granulated sugar, 1 teaspoon ground cinnamon
- UK: 120ml water, 60g unsalted butter, 2 tablespoons granulated sugar, 1/4 teaspoon salt, 120g all-purpose flour, 1 egg, 1/2 teaspoon vanilla extract, olive oil spray, 60g granulated sugar, 1 teaspoon ground cinnamon

Instructions:
1. In a saucepan, bring water, unsalted butter, granulated sugar, and salt to a boil.
2. Remove the saucepan from heat and stir in all-purpose flour until a dough forms.
3. Let the dough cool slightly, then beat in egg and vanilla extract until smooth.
4. Transfer the dough to a piping bag fitted with a star tip.
5. Preheat your air fryer to 180°C (350°F). Lightly grease the air fryer basket with olive oil spray.
6. Pipe strips of dough directly into the air fryer basket, cutting them with scissors or a knife.
7. Air fry the churros for 8-10 minutes until golden and crispy.
8. In a shallow bowl, mix granulated sugar and ground cinnamon.
9. Once the churros are done, immediately toss them in the cinnamon sugar mixture to coat.
10. Serve the air-fried cinnamon sugar churros warm as a delicious dessert or snack.

Nutritional Info (per serving):   Calories: 250 | Fat: 10g | Carbs: 35g | Protein: 3g

Raspberry Coconut Macaroons

Prep: 15 mins | Cook: 20 mins | Makes: 12 macaroons

Ingredients:
- US: 200g shredded coconut, 120ml maple syrup, 60ml coconut oil (melted), 1 teaspoon vanilla extract, 60g almond flour, 120g fresh raspberries, 60g dairy-free chocolate chips (optional)
- UK: 200g shredded coconut, 120ml maple syrup, 60ml coconut oil (melted), 1 teaspoon vanilla extract, 60g almond flour, 120g fresh raspberries, 60g dairy-free chocolate chips (optional)

Instructions:
1. Preheat your oven to 180°C (350°F). Line a baking sheet with parchment paper and set aside.
2. In a mixing bowl, combine shredded coconut, maple syrup, melted coconut oil, vanilla extract, and almond flour until well combined.
3. Gently fold in fresh raspberries until evenly distributed.
4. Use a cookie scoop or your hands to form the mixture into compact balls and place them on the prepared baking sheet.
5. If desired, press a few dairy-free chocolate chips onto the tops of the macaroons.
6. Bake for 18-20 minutes until the macaroons are golden brown and slightly firm to the touch.
7. Allow the raspberry coconut macaroons to cool completely on the baking sheet before serving.
8. Enjoy these delightful treats as a sweet snack or dessert.

Nutritional Info (per serving): Calories: 200 | Fat: 15g | Carbs: 20g | Protein: 2g

Chocolate Chip Chickpea Cookies

Prep: 15 mins | Cook: 12 mins | Makes: 12 cookies

Ingredients:
- US: 240g canned chickpeas (drained and rinsed), 60ml maple syrup, 60g almond butter, 1 teaspoon vanilla extract, 1/4 teaspoon baking powder, pinch of salt, 60g dairy-free chocolate chips
- UK: 240g canned chickpeas (drained and rinsed), 60ml maple syrup, 60g almond butter, 1 teaspoon vanilla extract, 1/4 teaspoon baking powder, pinch of salt, 60g dairy-free chocolate chips

Instructions:
1. Preheat your oven to 180°C (350°F). Line a baking sheet with parchment paper and set aside.
2. In a food processor, combine chickpeas, maple syrup, almond butter, vanilla extract, baking powder, and a pinch of salt.
3. Blend until smooth and creamy, scraping down the sides as needed.
4. Transfer the mixture to a bowl and fold in dairy-free chocolate chips.
5. Use a cookie scoop or your hands to form the mixture into balls and place them on the prepared baking sheet.
6. Flatten each ball slightly with the back of a spoon or your fingers.
7. Bake for 10-12 minutes until the edges are golden brown.
8. Allow the chocolate chip chickpea cookies to cool on the baking sheet for 5 minutes before transferring them to a wire rack to cool completely.
9. Enjoy these nutritious cookies as a guilt-free treat or snack.

Nutritional Info (per serving): Calories: 150 | Fat: 6g | Carbs: 20g | Protein: 4g

CHAPTER 10: SAUCES, DIPS, AND CONDIMENTS

Air-Fried Veggie Dips (Spinach Artichoke, Pico de Gallo, Hummus)
Prep: 15 mins | Cook: 15 mins | Serves: 6
Ingredients:
- US: For Spinach Artichoke Dip: 200g frozen spinach (thawed and drained), 200g canned artichoke hearts (chopped), 120g cream cheese, 60g sour cream, 60g mayonnaise, 60g grated Parmesan cheese, 2 cloves garlic (minced), salt, pepper
- For Pico de Gallo: 2 tomatoes (diced), 1/2 red onion (finely chopped), 1 jalapeño (seeded and minced), 1/4 cup fresh cilantro (chopped), 1 lime (juiced), salt, pepper
- For Hummus: 240g canned chickpeas (drained and rinsed), 2 cloves garlic, 30ml lemon juice, 30ml tahini, 30ml olive oil, salt, pepper
- UK: For Spinach Artichoke Dip: 200g frozen spinach (thawed and drained), 200g canned artichoke hearts (chopped), 120g cream cheese, 60g sour cream, 60g mayonnaise, 60g grated Parmesan cheese, 2 cloves garlic (minced), salt, pepper
- For Pico de Gallo: 2 tomatoes (diced), 1/2 red onion (finely chopped), 1 jalapeño (seeded and minced), 1/4 cup fresh coriander (chopped), 1 lime (juiced), salt, pepper
- For Hummus: 240g canned chickpeas (drained and rinsed), 2 cloves garlic, 30ml lemon juice, 30ml tahini, 30ml olive oil, salt, pepper

Instructions:
1. For Spinach Artichoke Dip: Preheat your air fryer to 180°C (360°F). In a bowl, mix together thawed and drained spinach, chopped artichoke hearts, cream cheese, sour cream, mayonnaise, minced garlic, grated Parmesan cheese, salt, and pepper. Transfer the mixture to an oven-safe dish and air fry for 12-15 minutes until bubbly and golden brown.
2. For Pico de Gallo: In a bowl, combine diced tomatoes, finely chopped red onion, minced jalapeño, chopped fresh cilantro, lime juice, salt, and pepper. Mix well and let the flavors meld for at least 15 minutes before serving.
3. For Hummus: In a food processor, combine drained and rinsed chickpeas, garlic cloves, lemon juice, tahini, olive oil, salt, and pepper. Blend until smooth and creamy, adding a splash of water if needed to reach desired consistency. Serve the hummus with a drizzle of olive oil and a sprinkle of paprika.

Nutritional Info (per serving - for each dip)

Mango Chutney
Prep: 10 mins | Cook: 20 mins | Serves: 8
Ingredients:
- US: 2 large ripe mangoes (peeled and diced), 1/2 cup apple cider vinegar, 1/2 cup brown sugar, 1/2 cup raisins, 1/2 onion (finely chopped), 2 cloves garlic (minced), 1 tablespoon fresh ginger (minced), 1 teaspoon mustard seeds, 1/2 teaspoon ground cinnamon, 1/4 teaspoon ground cloves, 1/4 teaspoon ground turmeric, salt
- UK: 2 large ripe mangoes (peeled and diced), 120ml apple cider vinegar, 100g brown sugar, 100g raisins, 1/2 onion (finely chopped), 2 cloves garlic (minced), 1 tablespoon fresh ginger (minced), 1 teaspoon mustard seeds, 1/2 teaspoon ground cinnamon, 1/4 teaspoon ground cloves, 1/4 teaspoon ground turmeric, salt

Instructions:
1. In a saucepan, combine diced mangoes, apple cider vinegar, brown sugar, raisins, chopped onion, minced garlic, minced ginger, mustard seeds, ground cinnamon, ground cloves, ground turmeric, and a pinch of salt.
2. Bring the mixture to a boil over medium heat, then reduce the heat and simmer for 15-20 minutes, stirring occasionally, until the chutney thickens.
3. Remove from heat and let the mango chutney cool completely before transferring to sterilized jars. Store in the refrigerator for up to 2 weeks.

Nutritional Info (per serving): Calories: 120 | Fat: 0.5g | Carbs: 30g | Protein: 1g

Pesto Sauce (Basil, Arugula, Sun-Dried Tomato)

Prep: 10 mins | Cook: 0 mins | Serves: 8

Ingredients:
- US: For Basil Pesto: 2 cups fresh basil leaves, 2 cloves garlic, 1/4 cup pine nuts, 1/2 cup grated Parmesan cheese, 1/2 cup olive oil, salt, pepper
- For Arugula Pesto: 2 cups fresh arugula leaves, 2 cloves garlic, 1/4 cup walnuts, 1/2 cup grated Parmesan cheese, 1/2 cup olive oil, salt, pepper
- For Sun-Dried Tomato Pesto: 1 cup sun-dried tomatoes (drained), 2 cloves garlic, 1/4 cup almonds, 1/2 cup grated Parmesan cheese, 1/2 cup olive oil, salt, pepper
- UK: For Basil Pesto: 2 cups fresh basil leaves, 2 cloves garlic, 25g pine nuts, 50g grated Parmesan cheese, 120ml olive oil, salt, pepper
- For Arugula Pesto: 2 cups fresh arugula leaves, 2 cloves garlic, 25g walnuts, 50g grated Parmesan cheese, 120ml olive oil, salt, pepper
- For Sun-Dried Tomato Pesto: 100g sun-dried tomatoes (drained), 2 cloves garlic, 25g almonds, 50g grated Parmesan cheese, 120ml olive oil, salt, pepper

Instructions:
1. For each pesto variation, combine fresh herbs or sun-dried tomatoes, garlic cloves, nuts, grated Parmesan cheese, olive oil, salt, and pepper in a food processor.
2. Blend until smooth, scraping down the sides of the processor bowl as needed, until you reach the desired consistency.
3. Taste and adjust seasoning if necessary.
4. Transfer the pesto to a jar and store it in the refrigerator for up to one week, or freeze it in ice cube trays for longer storage.

Nutritional Info (per serving - for each pesto):

Vegan Ranch Dressing

Prep: 10 mins | Cook: 0 mins | Serves: 8

Ingredients:
- US: 1 cup vegan mayonnaise, 1/2 cup unsweetened plant-based milk, 1 tablespoon apple cider vinegar, 1 teaspoon dried dill, 1 teaspoon dried parsley, 1/2 teaspoon garlic powder, 1/2 teaspoon onion powder, salt, pepper
- UK: 240ml vegan mayonnaise, 120ml unsweetened plant-based milk, 15ml apple cider vinegar, 5ml dried dill, 5ml dried parsley, 2.5ml garlic powder, 2.5ml onion powder, salt, pepper

Instructions:
1. In a bowl, whisk together vegan mayonnaise, plant-based milk, apple cider vinegar, dried dill, dried parsley, garlic powder, onion powder, salt, and pepper until smooth and creamy.
2. Taste and adjust seasoning according to preference.
3. Transfer the vegan ranch dressing to a jar and store it in the refrigerator for up to one week.

Nutritional Info (per serving): Calories: 80 | Fat: 8g | Carbs: 2g | Protein: 0g

Chipotle Cashew Cream Sauce

Prep: 10 mins | Cook: 0 mins | Serves: 6

Ingredients:
- US: 1 cup raw cashews (soaked in hot water for 1 hour), 1 chipotle pepper in adobo sauce, 2 tablespoons adobo sauce (from the chipotle peppers), 1/4 cup water, 2 tablespoons lime juice, 1 clove garlic, salt
- UK: 120g raw cashews (soaked in hot water for 1 hour), 1 chipotle pepper in adobo sauce, 30ml adobo sauce (from the chipotle peppers), 60ml water, 30ml lime juice, 1 clove garlic, salt

Instructions:
1. Drain the soaked cashews and rinse them under cold water.
2. In a blender, combine soaked cashews, chipotle pepper, adobo sauce, water, lime juice, garlic, and a pinch of salt.
3. Blend until smooth and creamy, adding more water if needed to reach the desired consistency.
4. Taste and adjust seasoning if necessary.
5. Transfer the chipotle cashew cream sauce to a jar and store it in the refrigerator for up to one week.

Nutritional Info (per serving): Calories: 100 | Fat: 8g | Carbs: 5g | Protein: 3g

Tzatziki Sauce

Prep: 10 mins | Cook: 0 mins | Serves: 6

Ingredients:
- US: 1 cup Greek yogurt, 1/2 cucumber (peeled, seeded, and grated), 1 clove garlic (minced), 1 tablespoon lemon juice, 1 tablespoon chopped fresh dill, 1 tablespoon chopped fresh mint, salt, pepper
- UK: 240ml Greek yogurt, 1/2 cucumber (peeled, seeded, and grated), 1 clove garlic (minced), 15ml lemon juice, 15ml chopped fresh dill, 15ml chopped fresh mint, salt, pepper

Instructions:
1. Place the grated cucumber in a clean kitchen towel and squeeze out excess moisture.
2. In a bowl, combine Greek yogurt, grated cucumber, minced garlic, lemon juice, chopped fresh dill, chopped fresh mint, salt, and pepper.
3. Mix until well combined.
4. Taste and adjust seasoning according to preference.
5. Transfer the tzatziki sauce to a jar and store it in the refrigerator for up to one week.

Nutritional Info (per serving): Calories: 40 | Fat: 1g | Carbs: 3g | Protein: 3g

Romesco Sauce

Prep: 15 mins | Cook: 10 mins | Serves: 8

Ingredients:
- US: 1 cup roasted red peppers (drained), 1/2 cup almonds (toasted), 2 cloves garlic, 2 tablespoons tomato paste, 2 tablespoons red wine vinegar, 1 teaspoon smoked paprika, 1/4 cup olive oil, salt, pepper
- UK: 240ml roasted red peppers (drained), 60g almonds (toasted), 2 cloves garlic, 30ml tomato paste, 30ml red wine vinegar, 5ml smoked paprika, 60ml olive oil, salt, pepper

Instructions:
1. In a food processor, combine roasted red peppers, toasted almonds, minced garlic, tomato paste, red wine vinegar, smoked paprika, salt, and pepper.
2. Pulse until the mixture is smooth.
3. With the food processor running, drizzle in olive oil until the sauce reaches the desired consistency.
4. Taste and adjust seasoning if necessary.
5. Transfer the romesco sauce to a jar and store it in the refrigerator for up to one week.

Nutritional Info (per serving): Calories: 120 | Fat: 10g | Carbs: 6g | Protein: 3g

Vegan Cheese Sauce

Prep: 10 mins | Cook: 5 mins | Serves: 6

Ingredients:
- US: 1 cup raw cashews (soaked in hot water for 1 hour), 1 cup unsweetened plant-based milk, 1/4 cup nutritional yeast, 2 tablespoons tapioca flour, 2 tablespoons lemon juice, 1 teaspoon garlic powder, 1/2 teaspoon onion powder, salt, pepper
- UK: 240g raw cashews (soaked in hot water for 1 hour), 240ml unsweetened plant-based milk, 30g nutritional yeast, 30g tapioca flour, 15ml lemon juice, 5ml garlic powder, 2.5ml onion powder, salt, pepper

Instructions:
1. Drain the soaked cashews and rinse them under cold water.
2. In a blender, combine soaked cashews, plant-based milk, nutritional yeast, tapioca flour, lemon juice, garlic powder, onion powder, salt, and pepper.
3. Blend until smooth.
4. Transfer the mixture to a saucepan and cook over medium heat, stirring constantly, until the sauce thickens.
5. Taste and adjust seasoning if necessary.
6. Serve the vegan cheese sauce immediately as a dip, sauce, or topping.

Nutritional Info (per serving): Calories: 150 | Fat: 10g | Carbs: 10g | Protein: 6g

Harissa Paste

Prep: 10 mins | Cook: 0 mins | Serves: 10

Ingredients:
- US: 8 dried red chili peppers (soaked in hot water for 30 minutes), 2 cloves garlic, 1 teaspoon ground cumin, 1 teaspoon ground coriander, 1/2 teaspoon caraway seeds, 2 tablespoons olive oil, 1 tablespoon tomato paste, 1 tablespoon lemon juice, salt
- UK: 8 dried red chili peppers (soaked in hot water for 30 minutes), 2 cloves garlic, 5ml ground cumin, 5ml ground coriander, 2.5ml caraway seeds, 30ml olive oil, 15ml tomato paste, 15ml lemon juice, salt

Instructions:
1. Drain the soaked red chili peppers and remove the stems.
2. In a food processor, combine soaked chili peppers, minced garlic, ground cumin, ground coriander, caraway seeds, olive oil, tomato paste, lemon juice, and a pinch of salt.
3. Blend until smooth, scraping down the sides of the processor bowl as needed.
4. Taste and adjust seasoning if necessary.
5. Transfer the harissa paste to a jar and store it in the refrigerator for up to one month.

Nutritional Info (per serving): Calories: 30 | Fat: 3g | Carbs: 1g | Protein: 0g

Air-Fried Veggie Croutons for Soups and Salads

Prep: 5 mins | Cook: 10 mins | Serves: 4

Ingredients:
- US: 4 slices whole wheat bread, 2 tablespoons olive oil, 1 teaspoon garlic powder, 1 teaspoon dried Italian herbs, salt, pepper
- UK: 4 slices whole wheat bread, 30ml olive oil, 5ml garlic powder, 5ml dried Italian herbs, salt, pepper

Instructions:
1. Preheat your air fryer to 180°C (360°F).
2. Cut the bread slices into cubes.
3. In a bowl, toss the bread cubes with olive oil, garlic powder, dried Italian herbs, salt, and pepper until evenly coated.
4. Spread the seasoned bread cubes in a single layer in the air fryer basket.
5. Air fry for 8-10 minutes, shaking the basket halfway through cooking, until the croutons are golden and crispy.
6. Remove the air-fried croutons from the air fryer and let them cool before serving.
7. Enjoy the crunchy goodness of these homemade veggie croutons in your soups and salads!

Nutritional Info (per serving): Calories: 100 | Fat: 6g | Carbs: 10g | Protein: 2g

CONCLUSION

As you reach the end of this "Vegetarian Air Fryer Cookbook UK," you've undoubtedly gained a wealth of knowledge, inspiration, and practical skills to embark on a journey of delicious, healthy, and sustainable vegetarian cooking. The combination of air frying and plant-based cuisine has proven to be a powerful one, opening up a world of endless possibilities for creating mouthwatering dishes that nourish both your body and soul.

Throughout these pages, we've explored the countless benefits of vegetarian air fryer cooking, from its positive impact on personal health and the environment to the incredible depth of flavors and textures it unlocks. By embracing this innovative cooking technique and the vibrant world of plant-based ingredients, you've taken a significant step towards a more mindful and fulfilling culinary experience. Reflect on how far you've come, from the initial curiosity about air frying to the newfound confidence and expertise you've acquired. Each recipe you've tackled has been a learning experience, teaching you valuable techniques, flavor combinations, and the art of transforming simple ingredients into extraordinary dishes. Whether you're a seasoned vegetarian chef or a newcomer to this lifestyle, you've undoubtedly expanded your culinary horizons and discovered a newfound appreciation for the versatility and deliciousness of plant-based fare. As you move forward, carry with you the knowledge that vegetarian air fryer cooking is not just a fleeting trend but a sustainable and rewarding lifestyle choice. The recipes and techniques you've mastered in this cookbook will serve as a solid foundation upon which you can continue to build and experiment. Don't be afraid to venture outside of these pages, exploring new ingredients, flavor profiles, and culinary traditions from around the world.

Remember, cooking is not just a practical pursuit but also a creative outlet and a means of connecting with others through shared flavors and traditions. Invite your friends and family to join you on this journey, sharing the joy and satisfaction of creating delicious, nourishing meals together. Encourage them to embrace the health benefits, environmental consciousness, and sheer enjoyment that comes with adopting a vegetarian, air fryer-friendly lifestyle. Celebrate the small victories along the way, whether it's mastering the perfect air-fried falafel, discovering a new favorite vegetable dish, or simply feeling more energized and vibrant as a result of your dietary choices. Every step you take towards a healthier, more sustainable lifestyle is a step worth acknowledging and appreciating.

As you continue to explore the world of vegetarian air fryer cooking, remember to stay curious, open-minded, and willing to adapt. Dietary preferences and restrictions may evolve, new ingredients and techniques may emerge, and your personal goals and motivations may shift. Embrace this fluidity, and let it fuel your passion for continuous learning and growth in the kitchen.

Moreover, don't forget to share your own experiences, tips, and culinary creations with others. Whether it's through social media, food blogs, or good old-fashioned conversations with friends and family, your unique perspective and insights can inspire and empower others to embark on their own vegetarian air fryer journeys. Finally, take pride in the fact that you've not only acquired a new set of culinary skills but also contributed to a larger movement towards sustainable living and conscious consumption. Every plant-based meal you prepare and every dish you air fry is a small yet significant step towards reducing your environmental impact and promoting a healthier planet for generations to come. As you close this cookbook, let it serve as a reminder of the incredible potential that lies within the combination of vegetarian cuisine and air frying. Carry with you the knowledge, inspiration, and passion you've gained, and let it fuel your ongoing exploration of delicious, nourishing, and sustainable meals. Embrace the joy of cooking, the power of plant-based ingredients, and the convenience of air frying, and watch as your culinary horizons expand in ways you never imagined.

Congratulations on embarking on this transformative journey, and may the recipes and principles you've learned in this "Vegetarian Air Fryer Cookbook UK" guide you towards a lifetime of flavorful, healthy, and deeply satisfying plant-based meals. Bon appétit!

Printed in Great Britain
by Amazon